# Christianity: Ethics

Sheila Butler

Philip Allan Updates, an imprint of Hodder Education, an Hachette UK company, Market Place, Deddington, Oxfordshire OX15 0SE

*Orders*

Bookpoint Ltd, 130 Milton Park, Abingdon, Oxfordshire OX14 4SB

tel: 01235 827827

fax: 01235 400401

e-mail: education@bookpoint.co.uk

Lines are open 9.00 a.m.–5.00 p.m., Monday to Saturday, with a 24-hour message answering service. You can also order through the Philip Allan Updates website: www.philipallan.co.uk

©Philip Allan Updates 2009

ISBN 978-0-340-98656-1

Impression number    6
Year    2014

All photographs are reproduced by permission of TopFoto, with the exception of those otherwise credited.

Printed in Italy

Hachette UK's policy is to use papers that are natural, renewable and recyclable products and made from wood grown in sustainable forests. The logging and manufacturing processes are expected to conform to the environmental regulations of the country of origin.

P1955

# Contents

# Contents

# Personal responsibility

# Social responsibility

## Global concerns

## Conflict

# Contents

# Introduction

This book gives you the information and guidance you need to be successful in the AQA GCSE Religious Studies Specification A Unit 2 exam, whether Short or Full Course. The title of this unit is 'Christianity: Ethics'.

The book covers all areas of the specification, in the same order as the specification. Where appropriate, the set topics are studied from different denominational perspectives.

## The exam

Success in the exam is not just about what you know and understand. It also depends on having the right exam technique. Some questions (usually the shorter ones) require purely factual answers. Others require an ability to apply Christian beliefs to the moral issues set for study. There is guidance on exam technique towards the end of this book. You should refer to this throughout your course, particularly when you write answers to essay questions.

## Using this book

This book is divided into sections covering each of the set topics. Each section follows the same format and provides the information you need to tackle any questions you might be set. As each issue is studied, reference will be made to biblical passages that some Christians use as guidance in deciding what is the morally right or wrong decision to make or action to take in relation to that issue. There will also be reference to the beliefs and teachings of different Christian denominations, such as those in the Catechism of the Catholic Church. There are no set biblical passages or Church teachings, but you should be able to show how some of these influence Christian attitudes to the topics being studied. It is essential that you understand a variety of Christian viewpoints and teachings on the set topics, whether or not you agree with them, and that your own views on them are carefully thought out.

At the end of each section on the topics there are various features:
- **Sample questions and answers** are intended to show you the kind of question you might be asked in an exam and the standard of answer to aim at.

- **Further questions** are for you to use as exam practice and to help you acquire the right technique.
- **Class activities** are intended for you to complete individually, in pairs or groups, under the direction of your teacher, to add breadth to your knowledge and depth to your understanding.
- **Homework** — for some of these tasks you will need access to the internet.
- **Useful websites** are appropriate to the section topic.

Section 1 is a short introductory section that outlines ways in which Christians approach moral decision-making and the sources of moral authority they might use. Although no questions are set on sources of moral authority in the exam, you are expected to understand the difference between absolute and relative approaches to moral decision-making in the topics set for study. So although no questions are set at the end of this introductory section, reading it and doing the activities at the end of it will help you with everything that follows.

At the end of the book there are a glossary and a list of websites that are generally relevant for the course. You will find the glossary useful for reference and revision of key words and definitions.

# Section 1

# Ways in which Christians make moral decisions

To a certain extent, the approach that all humans, Christians included, take to moral decision-making depends on how they see things generally. Some people have fixed ideas — things are either good or bad or right or wrong whatever the circumstances. Their opinions do not change. When it comes to ethics, this approach is known as **absolute morality**. Many people, however, have a more flexible and open approach to life. They may think that something is usually right or wrong, but that in some circumstances rules should be broken and a different decision should be made. This is known as **relative morality**. Others take this even further and think that there is no generally applicable standard on what is right and wrong. Each situation has to be considered separately and independently of rules or previous situations. The Christian theory known as Situation Ethics claims that people should take whatever is the most loving action in each situation. The slogan of Situation Ethics is 'love plus the situation'.

## Key words

**Absolute morality**
A type of morality that has fixed and unchanging rules

**Relative morality**
A type of morality that takes the situation and circumstances into account

# Sources of morality

Sometimes when you are faced with having to make a moral decision, there is no problem. It is clear what you should do. However, at other times you may be faced with a really difficult dilemma. In such situations you might need guidance or advice. You might ask your parents or friends, or you might rely on past experience. There are many sources of possible guidance. Christians might seek guidance and justify their actions from one or more of the following sources.

## The Bible

The Bible, and especially the New Testament, is a sacred text. This means that Christians believe it has special authority and respect its teachings and guidance. It is regarded as the word of God, but Christians understand this in different ways.

### Key words

**Christian denominations**
The different Christian traditions, e.g. Anglican, Roman Catholic

**Fundamentalist Christian**
Someone who believes that the Bible was inspired directly by God and contains no errors; its teachings are always relevant

**Liberal Christian**
Someone who believes that God guided the writers of the Bible, but that there are mistakes and some of its teachings are out of date

Some believe that those who wrote the books contained in the Bible were directly inspired by God, and that the teachings of Jesus and Paul in particular are to be followed absolutely by all Christians at all times. They adopt a **fundamentalist Christian** approach. Others take a more **liberal Christian** approach, believing that the writers were guided by God rather than directly inspired by him. God did not override their human limitations and sometimes they got it wrong. Liberal Christians believe that some of the Bible's teachings, laws and rules are outdated, so they need to be adapted or abandoned altogether.

## Religious leaders

Most **Christian denominations** have leaders who are regarded as experts in understanding and explaining the Bible. For Roman Catholics, the pope is an important source of moral guidance and a role model. The current pope is Benedict XVI.

Throughout the centuries there have been Christians who have devoted themselves to the service of others and who are sources of inspiration. You will read about some of them in this book.

Pope Benedict XVI

## Church teaching

This is important for many Christians, especially Roman Catholics. Many documents written or approved by the pope set out central beliefs and teachings that all Roman Catholics are expected to obey. Some deal with specific issues, such as the Vatican Declaration on Euthanasia. Others, such as the **Catechism of the Catholic Church**, cover every aspect of the faith.

### Key word

**Catechism of the Catholic Church**
A book containing the official teaching of the Roman Catholic Church on all matters of faith and practice

Other denominations also produce documents that set out thinking on key issues. For example, in recent decades the Anglican Church has produced reports relating to euthanasia, urban poverty, nuclear weapons and stem cell cloning.

## Reason

Many Christians believe they should use their minds to think through problems so that they are not swayed by emotions in issues like abortion. This is especially important if the Bible needs to be interpreted or if it does not contain guidance on the issue.

## Conscience

Many Christians think conscience is a moral guide — something that helps them to make the right decisions and that makes them feel guilty if they choose the wrong path. Many also believe it is something that develops as they mature and as a result of their upbringing and education.

# Questions and activities

## Class activities and homework

### Absolute and relative morality

In 2000, Siamese twins, Jodie and Mary, were born in Manchester. If they were left conjoined, they would survive only for a few months. If they were separated, Jodie would probably survive although she would need surgery and might be disabled, but Mary would certainly die. The doctors wanted to separate the twins but the parents opposed it. Three judges were given the task of deciding the outcome. In small groups, find out about this case and read the points made by the doctors and appeal judges. Then discuss the following questions and, under the supervision of your teacher, feed back your answers to the rest of the class. You will find the information you need by using the search engine on http://news.bbc.co.uk.

a Why would those who believe in absolute morality argue it was wrong to separate Jodie and Mary?

**b** Why would most people who believe in relative morality support the separation? Why do you think some who believe in relative morality might not be so sure?

**c** What does your group think about this case?

'Parents should have the right to decide for their children. Doctors and lawyers should not interfere.' Do you agree? Give reasons for your answer, showing that you have thought about more than one point of view. Refer to Christian arguments in your answer.

## Sources of moral decision-making

In pairs, take an A3 sheet of paper. Write the title 'Ways in which to make moral decisions'. At the top left-hand corner, write 'Moral problem' and in the bottom right-hand corner 'Decision made'. Then write on different parts of the page the five most important sources of moral guidance that you would turn to in order of their importance. Write the most important nearest the top left-hand corner and the least important nearest the bottom right-hand corner. Draw a line from the top corner to the bottom, linking up those words with the moral sources you have chosen. Then on the sheet write more sources of moral authority that people turn to, but do not put a line through them. Be prepared to justify your selection to the rest of the class.

Explain how different approaches to the Bible (e.g. fundamentalist, liberal) might affect the way Christians use it when trying to make a moral decision. Give examples in your answer.

'You should always obey your conscience.' Do you agree? Give reasons for your answer, showing that you have thought about more than one point of view. Refer to Christian arguments in your answer.

## Useful websites

http://news.bbc.co.uk

www.request.org.uk

# The right to life

# Section 2

# Abortion

**Abortion** arouses strong emotions. It is easy to get swept away on either side of the debate, but that is to trivialise it. There are serious and strong arguments on both sides that you need to think about rationally. At the same time, you might like to consider whether your view might change if you were personally involved as a potential parent, relative or friend.

## The law in the UK

The 1967 Abortion Act was passed to stop dangerous 'back-street' abortions. This Act permitted abortion in certain situations. In 1990, some amendments and additions were made.

The law works on the principle of **viability**, so there is a cut-off time of 24 weeks for most abortions. The law currently stands as shown in Figure 2.1 overleaf.

### Key words

**Abortion**
The deliberate termination of a pregnancy

**Viability**
The point in development at which a baby could be born with some chance of independent survival

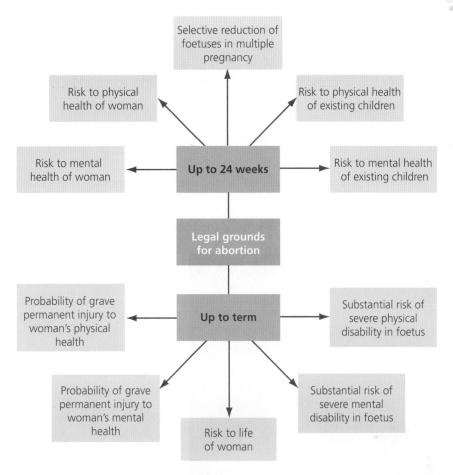

**Figure 2.1** The legal grounds for abortion

In practice, most abortions are carried out at a fairly early stage on the grounds of risk to the woman's mental health. **Foetal rights** are protected by the time limits contained in the Abortion Act. **Maternal rights** (the rights of the mother) and any existing children are also taken seriously. Doctors and nurses who are totally opposed to abortion do not have to carry out or assist in abortions. However, they must give post-abortion care. Doctors who are unwilling to sign a form allowing an abortion have to pass on their patients to doctors who have no such concerns. The law does not give any rights to potential fathers or personnel involved in the abortion process, such as medical secretaries.

## Reactions to the law

Many people would like to tighten up the procedure to prevent 'abortion on demand' and also to have the 24-week limit reduced. In 2008, however, Parliament voted against any such reduction.

Abortions are permitted later than 24 weeks if:

- the mother's life is at risk
- there is a risk of grave permanent injury to the mental or physical health of the mother
- there is a substantial risk that if the baby were born it would be severely disabled

Neil Bromhall/SPL

A 20-week-old foetus in the womb

However, many doctors are reluctant to perform abortions after 12 weeks. This is partly because by that stage everything is 'in place' — the rest of the pregnancy is largely a matter of growth and maturity of organs. Another reason is that the abortion procedure becomes more complex and distasteful beyond this point. Even more doctors are unhappy about performing abortions in the final **trimester**, especially if the grounds are disability.

In 2002, the late abortion of a foetus with a cleft palate led to a court case. There were strong opinions on either side.

### Key word

**Trimester**
A period of 3 months; pregnancy is divided into three trimesters

In contrast, some groups campaign for abortion on demand at any stage of pregnancy. They argue that the foetus has no rights until it is born, and that the woman is the best person to make a judgement. She has to carry and give birth to the baby. Feminists point out that the law was created by men. Why should they dictate what a woman may do in this most personal of situations?

Rev. Joanna Jepson took a health authority to court for allowing the late abortion of a foetus with a cleft lip and palate

# General arguments for and against abortion

Those who support abortion may offer the following reasons:

- The foetus is just a clump of cells or at best only a potential life.
- It is cruel to make a woman go through childbirth if she does not want the child.
- A teenage girl is not ready for the responsibilities of motherhood.
- A woman who has been raped should not have to cope with the product of rape growing and moving inside her.
- The abortion of a disabled foetus is in the best interests of everyone.
- No baby should be born into poverty, and it could make things even worse for the parents and any siblings.
- No child should be unwanted.
- Women have the right to dictate what happens to their bodies and they are the best ones to make an informed decision.

Those who oppose abortion may offer the following reasons:

- Life begins at conception so the embryo should have equal rights with the mother from the start. It deserves special protection because it is defenceless and vulnerable.
- Effective methods of contraception are available.
- Abortion may lead to terrible feelings of guilt.
- Abortion can cause long-term medical problems.
- It is wrong to punish a child conceived out of rape for the sin of its father.
- Disabled people are capable of fulfilled and happy lives, and support is available.
- Financial, material, emotional and spiritual support is available to mother and child.
- No child need be an unwanted child, but can be adopted.
- The right to **autonomy** is not absolute, especially when it involves harming another being. The woman's emotional involvement may prevent her making the wisest decision.

# Central issues about abortion

There are a number of issues at the heart of the abortion debate:

- Whose rights are the most important?
- When does life begin?
- Which matters most — sanctity of life or quality of life?

## Key words

**Autonomy**
The right to make decisions for yourself

**Pro-choice**
Supporting the right of women to decide for themselves whether or not to have an abortion

**Pro-life**
The anti-abortion view that the foetus has absolute right to life

## Whose rights are the most important?

**Pro-life** campaigners claim that foetal rights need absolute protection because a foetus is unable to defend itself. **Pro-choice** campaigners argue that maternal rights should come first. The mother is alive in a way that the foetus is not, and she alone has the right to make decisions about what happens in and to her body.

## When does life begin?

This issue is relevant for two reasons. First, being alive gives rights. Second, the deliberate killing of a living human is unlawful. To a certain extent, it depends on what you mean by 'life'. If you mean independent life, then it begins at birth because until then the foetus is entirely dependent on the woman carrying it. However, a baby is totally dependent on others, and so is a young child. A baby would not survive for long if it had to fend for itself.

Many people believe that life begins at conception, when something unique comes into being. Those who take this view speak of **ensoulment** or of the embryo being a human being. Others would say that the embryo is a *potential* person, so has some rights from the start, but that full rights are acquired as it develops. Many people see the development of the nervous system and brain activity as particularly significant.

### Key word

**Ensoulment**
The point at which the foetus receives its soul from God, and therefore becomes a person

Pro-life campaigners want to protect foetal rights

## Is sanctity of life more important than quality of life?

**Sanctity of life** means that life is sacred. It is special, precious and unique. Christians see life as God-given, and so it must be protected and respected. The term applies to both foetus and mother, though it is most often used in arguments against abortion.

### Key words

**Quality of life**
Whether or not a person will have a life that is worthwhile and of value

**Sanctity of life**
The idea that life is holy and precious

**Quality of life** refers to the kind of future the child will have when born. Will it be able to fulfil its potential? Is it wanted? Will it be loved? Will a severely disabled child lead a life full of suffering and frustration? The idea of quality of life is also applied to the mother, especially if she is young. Those who support abortion in some situations often do so on the grounds of quality of life.

# Christian attitudes to abortion

Although all Christians believe in the sanctity of life and take the issue of abortion seriously, there are differences of approach. Official Roman Catholic teaching absolutely opposes abortion, whereas many Protestants take a more relativist approach. There are, however, individual Roman Catholics who see abortion as justified in certain situations, and some Protestants who have a more absolutist approach.

## Roman Catholics

Roman Catholics take an absolute position, based on the sanctity of life principle. Abortion is much the same as murder: a grave sin meriting excommunication. Whether or not the embryo is fully a person at conception, it is entitled to full rights in view of the person it will become. From conception a human being is unique and infinitely precious in God's eyes. The Catechism of the Catholic Church and other Biblical texts support this view:

> My frame was not hidden from you when I was made in the secret place. When I was woven together in the depths of the earth, your eyes saw my unformed body. All the days ordained for me were written in your book before one of them came to be.          (Psalm 139:15–16)

Paralympic athlete Lucia Sosa from Mexico. Roman Catholics believe that God has a plan for every human life

Early Christian writings also support this anti-abortion stance. For example, the Didache (an early-second-century text) prohibits the killing of an unborn child.

The Catechism of the Catholic Church states: 'Human life must be respected and protected absolutely from the moment of conception' and that 'direct abortion…is gravely contrary to the moral law'.

By 'direct abortion', Roman Catholics mean actions intended to kill the foetus. However, they accept that some actions may be necessary to save the mother's life that result in the loss of the foetus. These are accepted as long as the intention is not to kill the foetus but to save maternal life.

Roman Catholics oppose abortion on the grounds of severe disability, believing that every life is of equal value and has potential and that it is not for humans to pass judgement on quality of life. They also state that it is unfair to punish the foetus for its father's sin in the case of rape, and that the birth of a child in such circumstances represents something good coming out of evil.

Roman Catholics stress the point that the alternatives to abortion should be taken seriously. For a woman who is certain that she does not want the child, it can be

adopted. In this way, a life is not destroyed; the child will be lovingly brought up by a couple who were longing for a child but unable to have one. For a mother willing to keep her child, there is good support both from the state and from the Christian community. This enables the mother to give her child a secure and loving upbringing. The Roman Catholic Church has many organisations, both local and national, that provide financial and emotional support for a mother, however young, to cope with pregnancy and looking after the baby.

## Anglicans

The Church of England agrees with the Roman Catholic Church that abortion is morally wrong, and is concerned about the number of abortions being performed. Nevertheless, in some circumstances compassion is central to the issue. Quality of life is taken into account, as well as sanctity of life. Anglicans accept abortion to save maternal life and many see it as justified in situations like rape. The official line on disability is that abortions after 24 weeks should only take place where the child would die soon after birth. Most Anglicans accept other types of severe disability as grounds for abortion up to 24 weeks if the mother feels it to be in the child's best interests. Above all, abortion is a matter of individual conscience.

## Methodists

Methodists see abortion as undesirable but believe that it is justified in cases of risk to the life or health of the mother and the existing family, and in cases of great poverty, rape and severe disability. It tries to strike a balance between sanctity and quality of life.

# Questions and activities

## Sample questions and answers

**1** What is an abortion? (1 mark)

 The deliberate termination of a pregnancy.

## Commentary

A short but clear definition is needed. There are other possible answers, e.g. the deliberate killing of a foetus. What matters is that you show the examiner that you know what the term means.

## 2 Explain why some Christians think abortion is always wrong.

(4 marks)

Christians believe that life is God-given and sacred, and some think this applies right from when the baby is conceived. To have an abortion is both a rejection of God's gift and an act of unlawful killing. The sixth Commandment (for Roman Catholics, the fifth) states 'Do not kill.' The foetus is especially vulnerable and defenceless, and has the right to protection. Some people would claim that to abort a disabled foetus would be an act of compassion, but many Christians would argue that humans do not have the right to make judgements on quality of life and that everyone is equally precious in the eyes of God. It is more compassionate to allow a disabled foetus as full a life as possible than to allow it no life at all.

## Commentary

This question is worth 4 marks and requires detailed discussion of a few points. A basic list giving four simple reasons would not receive more than 2 marks.

## 3 'The abortion of disabled babies should never be allowed.' Do you agree? Give reasons for your answer, showing that you have thought about more than one point of view. Refer to Christian teachings in your answer.

(6 marks)

Some people think it would be terrible for a mother to see her child grow up without fully developed limbs or with the mental age of a toddler. They think that, out of compassion for her, a foetus that is likely to suffer from disabilities should be aborted. They also think that such a child might suffer a lifetime of bullying and also of frustration at not being able to do the same things as its siblings and peers. Jesus said that one of the greatest commandments was to 'love your neighbour as yourself', and the New Testament stresses the importance of showing pity. Any pain suffered by the foetus would be short and preferable to what it would have to put up with if it were born.

I can see that such arguments do make some important points. For religious believers, compassion and love are essential qualities. Nobody likes to see a child suffer. Nevertheless, I do not agree with that view. I do not have any strong religious beliefs myself, but I think that at conception something totally unique comes into being with its own genetic structure. Life is sacred. Who are we to judge whether or not a disabled person can lead a worthwhile life? All he or she needs is love, respect and encouragement, which is what all humans need. Loving your neighbour and showing compassion mean enabling people to live to the full, not killing them before they have had the chance. If you watch the Paralympics, you can see that disabled people are no different from those without disability. They enjoy life just as much. Even if the baby's life is short, I think he or she should still have the chance. It is not cruel to the parents. It gives them the opportunity to love the being they have created, to say a proper farewell and to grieve. Many religious believers claim that only God has the right to say when life should end. I think it should end naturally, and not be given a helping hand.

## Commentary

This answer shows a different type of construction from that commonly used, where there was a paragraph on each side of the argument followed by a conclusion. Here, the way in which the answer is written means that there is no need for a conclusion. Nevertheless, as it considers two viewpoints, contains religious content and is well argued, it fulfils the criteria for Level 6, which means full marks.

## Further questions

1 Give two situations when the law would allow abortion.     (2 marks)
2 Explain why most Christians accept abortion if the woman's life is at risk.     (3 marks)
3 Do you think it is acceptable to use abortion as a form of contraception? Give reasons for your answer.     (4 marks)
4 Explain different ideas about when the foetus has rights.     (4 marks)

## Class activities and homework

### Joanna Jepson and the case of the cleft-palate abortion

In pairs, type 'Joanna Jepson' into Google and in the search box in the BBC News website at http://news.bbc.co.uk. Find out all you can about the case, and write some questions to put to an 'Any Questions' panel. The panel will consist of a chairperson, Joanna Jepson, a doctor, a representative from LIFE (an anti-abortion group) and a representative from Abortion Rights (which supports abortion on demand). Your teacher will choose five members of your class to take the roles of each of these people. They should research the case and work out what each person might have thought about it. Then hold an 'Any Questions' session.

Create a chart showing the different stages of foetal development. Using different colours and a colour key, mark the point (if you think there is one) at which the foetus is definitely a person, the point at which it is definitely not a person (again, if you think there is one) and the point at which you think the foetus is a person and should have rights.

### Pro-life/pro-choice magazine article

In pairs, create a magazine article of between 100 and 200 words, giving a pro-life or pro-choice view on abortion. You may structure and set out your article as you wish.

Find out and make detailed notes on different Christian viewpoints on abortion. Copy any relevant quotations and highlight the phrases that you would find it useful to learn. Underneath each quote, make a note of whether you would use it in support of or against abortion.

Use the information in this book and the notes you made for yourself to write two paragraphs explaining how Christian beliefs and teachings might affect a religious believer's attitude to abortion.

## Useful websites

www.abortionrights.org.uk

www.bbc.co.uk/ethics Click on *Abortion*.

http:news.bbc.co.uk Click on *Abortion*.

http://prolife.org.uk

www.request.org.uk Click on *Issues*, *A–Z of Issues* and *Abortion*.

http://re-xs.ucsm.ac.uk Click on *Ethical & Moral Issues*, then on *Abortion*.

www.spuc.org.uk Click on *Ethical Issues*, then on *Abortion*.

www.lifecharity.org.uk Click on *Education*, then on *Abortion*.

# Section 3

# Euthanasia

**Euthanasia** is an emotive topic. The word literally means 'good death' and is often explained as 'mercy killing' or 'dying with dignity'.

> **Key word**
>
> **Euthanasia**
> The deliberate termination of a life in order to end someone's suffering

Although euthanasia is legal in some countries such as the Netherlands, in the UK it is illegal. Those involved are at best charged with assisting suicide and at worst with murder. There were a number of high-profile cases towards the end of the twentieth century. Dr Nigel Cox was found guilty of attempted murder for injecting potassium chloride into an incurably ill elderly woman whose pain was intolerable, and who repeatedly begged him to end her life. Dr David Moor was acquitted of murder on the grounds that the high levels of morphine he gave to terminally ill patients were not intended to kill.

There have been many attempts to change the law, and MPs have been given a free vote on this, but the majority have always opposed it. Many doctors and nurses have serious concerns about legalising euthanasia, although surveys show that the general public supports it in certain situations.

Diane Pretty lost a court battle for the right to commit assisted suicide

## Key words

**Active euthanasia**
Deliberately ending the life of someone who is seriously ill

**Passive euthanasia**
Letting a person die without medical intervention

**Non-voluntary euthanasia**
Ending the life of a sick person who is incapable of requesting death

**Voluntary euthanasia**
Ending a person's life at his or her request

# Types of euthanasia

- **Voluntary euthanasia** is when a person asks a doctor to end his or her life.
- **Non-voluntary euthanasia** occurs when the patient is unable to request an end to life but it is believed to be in his or her best interests.

If voluntary euthanasia were legalised, it might be used in situations of:

- terminal or incurable and very painful illnesses
- degenerative diseases, which lead to loss of dignity and quality of life

If non-voluntary euthanasia were legalised, it might be used for:

- those in comas or incapable of communication
- severely disabled newborn babies
- people suffering from dementia

## Active and passive euthanasia

**Active euthanasia** is illegal in the UK. It is an action taken or withheld with the deliberate intention of ending someone's life.

**Passive euthanasia** is legal as there is no intention to kill. It may take two forms:

- A doctor gives a patient a pain-relieving drug such as morphine, knowing that the dosage will have to be increased as the patient develops tolerance of the drug, and knowing that it will shorten the patient's life. This is not illegal because the intention is to relieve pain, not to end life. It is seen as good medical practice and an example of the principle of double effect.

- Medical treatment may be withheld or withdrawn from a dying person on the grounds that it is wrong to prolong the natural process of dying. The intention is not to kill, but simply to acknowledge and allow the inevitable.

## The Dignity in Dying organisation

Dignity in Dying campaigns for the legalisation of voluntary euthanasia and for **advance decisions** (sometimes referred to as 'living wills'), in which people can state that if they lose all reasonable quality of life and are incapable of making their wishes known, they want their lives to be ended. People from all spheres of society are members, including medical personnel and religious leaders.

## The Pro-Life Alliance

This is the first European political party to be based on pro-life principles. It campaigns for the right to life as fundamental, and for more **hospices** to be properly funded to provide first-class care.

# The hospice movement

In the Middle Ages, Christian monks established hospices as resting places for weary travellers. The modern hospice movement provides a resting place for the terminally ill.

Most hospices are run by charities and care for anyone who needs their services, regardless of age, belief or culture. They are founded on the principles of compassion and loving service and on the basis that all people should be able to die with dignity, receiving the best possible care and absolute respect. The high staffing ratio means that people are treated as valued individuals.

### Key words

**Advance decisions**
Statements telling medical staff how patients wish to be treated at the end of their lives, should they be unable to communicate their wishes

**Hospice**
A place that provides care for terminally ill patients

**Palliative care**
Special care that gives relief from pain and other distressing aspects of terminal illness

Above all, hospices provide expert **palliative care**, which gives patients some quality of life right to the end. They also provide treatment and give counselling. Patients and their families are encouraged to talk about and prepare for death,

**Key word**

**Respite care**
A short period
of rest for
carers

with religious support available if they want it. The needs of the family are met both before and after death with counselling and group meetings. Some patients stay in the hospice until they die, while others go in for assessment or for **respite care**.

Some hospices provide only or primarily day care. There are specialist children's and teenagers' hospices, which have rooms for parents and siblings of patients who wish to stay for a short time. Cicely Saunders (the founder of the hospice movement) said that terminal care everywhere should become so good that no one would feel the need to request voluntary euthanasia.

Naomi House Children's Hospice in Sutton Scotney, Hampshire

*Zoe Klassnik/PA Archive/PA Photos*

# General arguments for and against euthanasia

The arguments in support of legalising voluntary euthanasia are:

- People have the right to choose, and the right to autonomy up to and including death.

- Euthanasia provides a quick and humane release from suffering. In similar circumstances we would choose euthanasia for our pets.
- Death is easier to face if we know it will be painless and dignified.
- Advance decisions can remove anxiety about the future.
- The suffering of relatives is lessened, and so is the burden of caring.
- The burden on the state is lessened.
- Doctors need not fear prosecution for carrying out euthanasia.

The arguments against legalising voluntary euthanasia are:

- It is unnecessary in view of the great advances made in palliative care in hospices and by **Macmillan nurses** at home.
- It is impossible to be sure that an individual wants to die if he or she cannot communicate.
- We cannot know how we will feel about things in the future.
- The last weeks and months of someone's life are helpful to relatives as a time for sharing affection and adapting to the fact that the loved one will not always be there.
- Unscrupulous relatives might abuse the system.
- Euthanasia implies that life is disposable.
- There could be a 'slippery slope' that would end up with a situation similar to that in Nazi Germany, where people were put to death without their consent, simply because the Nazis decided on it.
- Mistakes might be made.

Macmillan Cancer Support

A Macmillan nurse with a doctor. Macmillan nurses help people with cancer to enjoy a better quality of life

## Key word

**Macmillan nurse**
A nurse who is specially trained in palliative care for cancer patients

# Christian attitudes to euthanasia

All the mainstream Christian denominations in Britain have made official statements opposing active euthanasia. In addition to the general arguments given earlier, their reasons are:

- Life is sacred and God-given. Only God has the right to take it. He has a special purpose for each individual and nobody should interfere with his plan, however good their intentions.
- Euthanasia shows a lack of trust in God's love and mercy.
- God gave humans dominion over creation and the right to make responsible decisions for themselves, but there are limits to autonomy. To take life in this way is to play God.
- The weak and vulnerable who are unable to speak for themselves should have special protection.
- Euthanasia breaks the sixth Commandment (for Roman Catholics, the fifth) — do not kill.

The Vatican Declaration on Euthanasia states that euthanasia is: 'the violation of the divine law, an offence against the dignity of the human person, a crime against life, and an attack on humanity'. Nevertheless, many individual Christians believe that euthanasia should be legalised. In addition to the general arguments listed earlier, their reasons are:

- Life is sacred, but not absolutely so. It involves more than biological existence, and quality of life matters, too.
- Terrible suffering and loss of dignity are not what God wants for people. To put an end to these is working with God.
- God gave humans dominion over creation, which means being entrusted with responsible decision-making throughout life.
- Personal autonomy is a God-given right. People have the right to self-determination, i.e. to make responsible decisions for themselves. Although God's purposes should be respected, he created humans with the capacity for choice, so humans have the right to self-determination. They make responsible decisions for themselves in most areas of life, and this should include decisions about the way they die.

All Christians accept passive euthanasia if medical treatment would prolong the process of dying. The Roman Catholic Church opposes the removal of feeding tubes from patients in a **permanent vegetative state (PVS)**. Other Christians see artificial feeding as medical treatment and think it can be withdrawn.

> ### Key word
>
> **Permanent vegetative state (PVS)**
> An irreversible condition caused by the destruction of the neocortical area of the brain

# Questions and activities

## Sample questions and answers

**1** Which kind of nurses are specially trained in palliative care?

(1 mark)

Macmillan nurses.

### Commentary

A 1-mark question requires only a simple answer.

**2** Explain the 'slippery slope' argument against euthanasia.

(2 marks)

This argument claims that you may start by allowing only voluntary euthanasia, but it will not stop at that. It's a bit like a snowball rolling down a hill, which gets bigger and bigger. Eventually all kinds of euthanasia will be allowed.

### Commentary

This question is worth 2 marks, so a developed point is needed.

**3** Why do Christians disagree over withdrawing feeding tubes from PVS patients?

(4 marks)

Some Christians believe that this tube is a form of feeding, and patients always have the right to be fed. To remove it would be a callous act and tantamount to murder. It is a form of active, not passive, euthanasia. Other Christians, however, disagree. In PVS situations, all the tube does is prolong the dying. The person has no hope of recovery, and the feeding tube can be seen just as a piece of medical equipment. To remove it is responsible and compassionate, and an act of passive euthanasia.

## Commentary

This question requires two viewpoints to be given. Because each view is worth 2 marks, some development of points is needed.

**4** 'If Christians really believed in compassion, they would support euthanasia.' Do you agree? Give reasons for your answer, showing that you have thought about more than one point of view. Refer to Christian teachings in your answer.     (6 marks)

I don't agree with this at all. Life is sacred and precious in God's eyes. Giving someone a quality of life and the belief that his or her life has value right up to the end is far more compassionate than saying, 'Your life has no point. Wouldn't you be better off dead?' The hospice movement means that euthanasia isn't necessary. Pain can be relieved and death can be dignified. If patients want to die at home with family around them, Macmillan nurses are available to give support. It is also more compassionate for families, who will treasure those last weeks and days with their dying relatives instead of always wondering if they did the right thing, and whether the really important things had been said and done.

I can, however, see why some people would disagree with me. In his lifetime Jesus did what he could to remove suffering. He certainly did not try to prolong it. As palliative care was not available, he might have supported voluntary euthanasia, where someone suffering terrible pain from terminal illness just did not have the emotional strength to go on any more. After all, when our pets are ill, we take them to the vet to be put down, as we do not wish them to suffer further. Some people think that this compassionate and unselfish caring for animals should be extended to people. If the hospice movement did not exist, I might agree with this view. But it does, and so I believe that it is far more compassionate to give someone a reason to want to continue living.

## Commentary

This answer is totally focused on the question, which centres around compassion. It considers both sides of the argument and makes reference to religious views. All these features are essential if an evaluative answer is to gain full marks.

## Further questions

**1** What is meant by the term 'voluntary euthanasia'? (2 marks)

**2** Which Christian denomination supports voluntary euthanasia? (1 mark)

**3** Explain how some Christians use the idea of quality of life to support the argument for euthanasia. (4 marks)

**4** Explain how some Christians use the idea of sanctity of life to oppose the argument for euthanasia. (4 marks)

## Class activities and homework

### Euthanasia and assisted suicide

Your teacher will divide your class into groups and assign one of the following case studies to each group: Dr David Moor, Diane Pretty, Tony Bland, Heather Pratten, Anne Turner. You will be given the materials you need or will be able to do your own research on http://news.bbc.co.uk by searching for the name of the person you have been allocated. Prepare a short talk for the rest of the class, explaining the issues and whether you agree with the actions taken. (Although assisted suicide is not the same as euthanasia, the arguments for and against it are much the same, and so it is useful to study cases such as Diane Pretty.)

Note down your own views on the case study you were given.

### The hospice movement

If possible, your teacher will invite someone from a local hospice to talk about the hospice movement. Make sure you have thought about this meeting beforehand and have some questions ready. If no speaker is available your teacher will suggest useful websites for you to research the aims and facilities of hospices.

Find out about the case of Miss B by using the search engine on http://news.bbc.co.uk. Do you think her life-support machine should have been switched off? Justify your opinion.

## Useful websites

www.bbc.co.uk/ethics/euthanasia

www.dignityindying.org.uk

www.helpthehospices.org.uk

http://news.bbc.co.uk

http://prolife.org.uk Type *Euthanasia* into the search facility.

http://re-xs.ucsm.ac.uk Click on *Ethical & Moral Issues*, then on *Euthanasia*.

# The use of medical technology

# Section 4

# Fertility treatments

Advances in medical science in recent years have prompted many questions. What limits, if any, should be placed on it? If life is sacred, does that mean it is right for medical science to be used to help people have children? Is that correcting nature or interfering with it, and are both morally acceptable? How do beliefs about sanctity of life and when life begins influence views on embryonic research? As stated earlier in this book, Christians believe in the sanctity of life, but they differ in the conclusions that they draw from that belief; and there are also different opinions on responsibility for life.

Many couples long for a child but find that they are unable to have one through sexual intercourse. This causes immense suffering, but there are now alternative ways for a woman to become pregnant.

## Types of fertility treatment

Although there are many types of assisted conception that may be used in **fertility treatment**, you only need to know about three:

**Key word**

**Fertility treatment**
Treatment given to enable women to conceive

## 4

- **Artificial insemination by husband (AIH)**: the man's sperm is collected and inserted into the woman's cervix. Fertilisation is left to take place naturally.

- **Artificial insemination by donor/donor insemination (AID/DI)**: donors are paid a small sum to donate sperm to a sperm bank, after having been tested for HIV and other conditions that might be transmitted. The procedure used for AIH is then followed. The husband's or partner's name appears on the birth certificate. When children reach 18, they have the right to know the identity of their genetic fathers.

- **In vitro fertilisation (IVF)**: the woman's ovaries are hormonally stimulated and eggs are collected at ovulation. Sperm is collected and used to fertilise the eggs. The embryos are then checked for viability over a few days, and one or two placed into the woman's uterus in the hope that they will implant. The fate of any remaining viable embryos is decided by the couple concerned. They may be frozen in liquid nitrogen for future use, given to other infertile couples, donated for embryonic research, or destroyed. Current practice is that if the embryos are cryopreserved (frozen in liquid nitrogen) and not used within 5 years, the couple are asked what they want to happen to them. It must be a joint decision. Legislation still to be finalised would extend that period to 10 years.

## Key words

**Artificial insemination by donor/donor insemination (AID/DI)**
A form of fertility treatment using donor sperm

**Artificial insemination by husband (AIH)**
A form of fertility treatment using the husband's (or partner's) sperm

**In vitro fertilisation (IVF)**
A form of fertility treatment in which the eggs are fertilised outside the womb

Louise Brown, the first 'test-tube baby', who was born after IVF treatment

# Embryonic research

IVF treatment entails the creation of spare embryos. These may be used for research purposes, but there are strict rules regulating this:

- All research has to be licensed and is regulated by the **Human Fertilisation and Embryology Authority (HFEA)**. Embryonic research is only permitted if the HFEA is satisfied that it is necessary for one of a limited list of purposes, including improving knowledge about serious disease.
- The consent of both parents is needed.
- Research must be carried out within 14 days of an embryo being created because after this period the nervous system starts to form.

> **Key words**
>
> **Cloning**
> The technique used to produce a genetically identical copy of an organism
>
> **Genetic engineering**
> The modification of a person's genetic structure, usually to cure disease
>
> **Human Fertilisation and Embryology Authority (HFEA)**
> The body that oversees the use of embryos in fertility treatment and research

Roman Catholics oppose embryonic research for the same reasons as they oppose abortion. They believe that, right from conception, the embryo is a living being, loved by God and with the right to life. Additionally, they believe it has the absolute right to be treated with respect and to be protected from exploitation, so that not even the good intentions of relieving suffering and saving life can justify embryonic research. They regard the eventual destruction of these embryos as effectively murder, breaking the commandment not to kill.

Some Protestants agree with the Roman Catholic view, but many believe that in the early stages embryos are only potential humans, and that, although they have the right to respect, they may be used in research for the benefit of humanity, so long as:

- it does not continue beyond 14 days
- there is no other alternative
- it is solely for therapeutic reasons

Views on the status and use of the embryo affect attitudes not only to the use of IVF, but also to the procedures of human **genetic engineering** and **cloning**, which will be considered in the following sections.

# Surrogacy

As an alternative to standard fertility treatments, sometimes a woman carries and gives birth to a child on behalf of another couple. This is known as **surrogacy**. The woman agrees beforehand to give the baby to the couple to bring up. Surrogacy may be used if the commissioning woman (the woman wanting a baby) has a history of repeated miscarriages or if pregnancy would endanger her life. The two main types of surrogacy are:

**Key word**

**Surrogacy**
An alternative to standard fertility treatment, in which a woman who gives birth to a baby on behalf of another couple is not necessarily one of the genetic parents

- Partial surrogacy: the commissioning couple are also the genetic parents. The surrogate is simply the carrying mother.
- Total surrogacy: the commissioning man's sperm is artificially inseminated into the uterus of the surrogate, so that she is the genetic as well as the carrying mother.

Although surrogacy is legal, contracts between a couple and a surrogate mother are not enforceable. Whatever the type of surrogacy and however much the surrogate mother has been paid, she is the legal mother. She may decide to have an abortion, or to keep the baby after birth. At birth, the commissioning father can obtain equal legal rights with the surrogate mother, but the surrogate mother loses her claim to the child only if she signs a document to this effect after six weeks. Commercial surrogacy is illegal. Legally, the surrogate mother can be paid reasonable expenses only, but sometimes large sums of money have been involved.

Surrogate mother Kate Housley and her husband Dennis (left) with Fiona and Andrew O'Driscoll, genetic and commissioning parents of baby Hannah

# General arguments for and against fertility treatment

There are strong arguments in favour of fertility treatment:

- It shows compassion.
- It is just a form of medical treatment, restoring a natural function.
- It ensures justice for infertile couples, to whom nature has been unfair.
- The resulting child will feel especially wanted and loved because the parents went to great lengths to have a child.

There are, however, many arguments against:

- Fertility treatments are unnatural and are 'playing God'.
- A sperm donor may not want his personal life disrupted by the sudden appearance of a young person resulting from his act of generosity to a childless couple 18 years ago.
- There could be tensions between parents as a result of sperm or egg donation because only one parent is the genetic parent.
- A surrogate mother may bond with the child she is carrying, particularly if it is hers genetically, and she may suffer terribly from giving it up.
- There have been examples of IVF embryos being implanted into the wrong woman.
- IVF treatment is expensive, so is it a wise use of money when the National Health Service is so stretched?
- Problems arise if a couple split up and the woman wants another baby from frozen embryos, but her ex-partner objects.

# Christian views on fertility treatments

## Roman Catholics

The Roman Catholic Church understands the distress caused to couples who are unable to have children because of infertility and it supports research aimed at reducing it. At the same time, it rejects the idea of people having a right to have children. A child is a gift from God, in accordance with his purposes. The Catechism of the Catholic Church suggests that people should accept infertility as God's will for them and find fulfilment through adoption, fostering or some other way of helping others.

Assisted conception goes against natural law, which states that children should be produced by an act that is both unitive and procreative. Moreover, masturbation (needed to collect the sperm) is sinful. Nevertheless, the most recent Vatican Statement accepts forms of insemination that help the sexual relationship between the couple to achieve its purpose.

IVF is particularly sinful because of the spare embryos that are created and often used for research purposes before being destroyed. The 2008 Vatican Document 'The Dignity of a Person' is opposed to cryopreservation, but does not condemn outright the 'adoption' of spare embryos by another infertile couple.

Donor insemination brings a third party into the marriage and is 'mechanical adultery'. It may also create social and psychological problems for both the child and the parents.

Surrogacy is opposed for the reasons given above, and also because it is seen as reducing the 'mysterious' and wonderful process of conception and pregnancy to what has been described as a barnyard procedure.

## Protestants

Protestants usually accept fertility treatment for a number of reasons. One of the most important of these arises from the biblical teaching that children are a blessing. Children are thought to enrich a marriage, and so enabling the infertile to conceive is compassionate. The story of Hannah in 1 Samuel 1 illustrates just how distressing infertility is for those who experience it.

Protestants also believe that medical scientists have been given their skills by God and that overcoming infertility is a responsible use of the authority over nature that was given to humans at their creation. Creativity is part of what it means to be in the image of God (Genesis 1:26). Assisted conception (another term for fertility treatment) is not against nature; it is putting nature right. Protestants claim that assisted conception is like an extension of Jesus' healing power as seen in the Gospels. Had Jesus been on earth now, he would have supported it.

However, there are differences of opinion about donor insemination, with some Protestants sharing the Roman Catholic view. Others, though, regard sperm donation as just a means of fertilisation and not as mechanical adultery. Providing that donors are not paid (other than expenses), sperm donation is an act of love. Payment would lead to the **commercialisation** of human life. It would encourage greed and the treatment of babies as a commodity.

**Key word**

**Commercialisation**
Exploiting for the purpose of making a profit

Most Protestants are opposed to surrogacy as a general practice. They accept that the intention may be compassionate and loving, but worry about possible social and psychological problems for all concerned. Some Christians claim that the story of Hagar (Sarah's slave) bearing a child that then belonged to Abraham and Sarah is an example of surrogacy from the Old Testament (Genesis 16:1–16). Others disagree, saying it was a totally different scenario.

# Questions and activities

## Sample questions and answers

**1** Which organisation is in charge of giving licences for research on embryos? (1 mark)

 The HFEA.

### Commentary

The initials are sufficient.

**2** 'Surrogacy is an act of Christian compassion.' What do you think? Explain your opinion. (3 marks)

 I think this statement is absolutely true. It must be terrible for a woman who has repeated miscarriages. What could be kinder than taking pity on her and offering to carry her child, despite having to sacrifice nine months of your life? It is also showing compassion to those who will be the child's grandparents and who otherwise would be deprived of that joy. Jesus said that humans will be judged on how they treated others and I think he would have approved of this.

## Commentary

This question asks for a personal response to an issue that has religious significance. It does not demand the kind of balanced and detailed argument needed for 6-mark evaluations. It is important to focus on the statement and give sound reasons for your opinion on it. You do not need to give Christian views in great depth, but religious content is required because of the way in which the statement is phrased.

**3** Explain briefly why Roman Catholics oppose the use of in vitro fertilisation (IVF)  (3 marks)

Roman Catholics oppose it for several reasons. They believe that babies should be conceived naturally through sexual intercourse and not be the products of laboratory techniques. They disagree with the creation of spare embryos that might be destroyed or used in research as this is destroying human life that is God's gift.

## Further questions

**1** Why do embryos used for medical research have to be destroyed after 14 days?  (1 mark)
**2** Explain what is meant by artificial insemination by husband (AIH).  (2 marks)
**3** Explain two reasons why many people oppose surrogacy.  (4 marks)
**4** Explain Christian attitudes to donor insemination.  (4 marks)

## Class activities and homework

### Surrogacy

Your teacher will divide you into three groups, each of which will prepare a presentation on one of the following: the different types of surrogacy and who might need them; the criteria for becoming a surrogate mother; the law and surrogacy. Use the websites listed at the end of this section to help you.

In pairs, find out about Carole Horlock on the internet. Do you think she was right to ignore medical advice when it was discovered she was carrying triplets?

Using the COTS website (www.surrogacy.org.uk), read the testimonials of those who have acted as surrogates. Do they affect your views on surrogacy?

## Useful websites

www.surrogacy.org.uk

www.surrogacyuk.org

www.cofe.anglican.org Click on *About the Church*, then *Social and Public Issues, Science & Medical Ethics* and *Human Fertilisation & Embryology*.

www.ethicaldimension.org

www.cmf.org.uk Click on *Ethics & Issues*, then *Reproductive Technology*.

http://hcd2.bupa.co.uk/fact_sheets/html/assisted_conception.html

http://news.bbc.co.uk Key in *Fertility Treatment*.

# Human genetic engineering

Human genetic engineering is currently used to correct a faulty gene in a living person and also to create **saviour siblings**. It is usually referred to as gene therapy, as it is genetic engineering used for therapeutic reasons (i.e. to restore health). Some would also like to see genetic engineering developed for non-therapeutic purposes, to create 'designer babies'. This is controversial.

## Somatic-cell therapy

**Somatic-cell therapy** treats individuals by targeting non-reproductive cells, so any cure is only of the person treated and would not extend to any children he or she might have. In 2002, a toddler called Rhys Evans was treated for a genetic defect that causes lack of immunity to infection. In his case, a working copy of the gene that didn't work was inserted into his DNA. That treatment was successful and other children have since been treated for the same condition. In 2007, gene therapy was carried out on three young people with a particular form of childhood blindness. A year later, a significant improvement was noted in the case of one of them.

### Key words

**Saviour siblings**
Babies conceived using PGD and IVF so that their cord blood can be used to treat a seriously sick sibling

**Somatic-cell therapy**
A form of gene therapy that corrects a faulty gene

*Andrew Parsons/PA Archive/PA Photos*

The parents of desperately ill Zain Hashmi won the right to create a saviour sibling to treat him

## Saviour siblings

For a few years it has been possible to save the life of a child with a life-threatening disorder through the use of **pre-implantation genetic diagnosis (PGD)**. This involves screening embryos created in IVF treatment to select those that would be the closest match to the sick child. Suitable embryos are implanted in the mother. If there is a successful pregnancy and birth, the cord blood is used as a source of stem cells that can be transplanted into the older child.

### Key words

**Designer babies**
Babies whose genetic structure has been structured to ensure particular characteristics

**Pre-implantation genetic diagnosis (PGD)**
Screening embryos created in IVF treatment to select those that would be the closest match to a sick child

## Designer babies

Saviour siblings are often described as **designer babies** because their genetic make-up is selected to be as close as possible to that of the sick brother or sister. This is lawful, as is sex selection where there is a sex-linked genetic disorder. UK law does not permit sex selection for social reasons, however, nor does it support research into ways of enabling couples to choose their child's appearance, or his or her intellectual or sporting potential.

# General arguments for and against genetic engineering

There are strong arguments for genetic engineering:

- It is a compassionate response to disease.
- Parents should have the right to choose treatments for their children.
- Somatic-cell therapy is just an extension of everyday medical treatment.
- It may well be more effective and less expensive than other treatments.
- It saves lives and the benefits outweigh any risks.
- In the case of designer babies, it is natural for parents to want the best for a child. Why should parents not try to ensure they have super-intelligent, beautiful or sporty offspring?
- So long as the saviour sibling is wanted for himself or herself, there is nothing wrong in seeking to save the life of a seriously ill child through PGD. Saving life is good, and the baby is not being harmed in any way.

There are also strong arguments against such treatments:

- They are unnatural. Medical scientists are 'playing God'.
- There is fear of the slippery slope. What starts as somatic-cell therapy might lead ultimately to eugenics, i.e. selective breeding to ensure that only children with particular characteristics are born.
- There are big risks. A French boy treated in a similar way to Rhys Evans developed leukaemia.
- If designer babies ever became possible, it might be that only the rich could afford them. This would be an injustice.
- Designer babies could become big business. Children would then be seen simply as a commodity, something bought to order.
- The use of IVF to create genetically compatible siblings may save life, but will such children grow up to feel wanted, or feel that they were a means to an end? And if the treatment fails, there could be disastrous psychological effects on family relationships.

# Christian views on human genetic engineering

Views are mixed. There are serious concerns about 'playing God' and medical scientists interfering irreversibly with something they do not fully understand. The creation of designer babies is seen as idolatrous worship of qualities such as beauty or intellect. There are concerns about the commercialisation of medical treatment and the two-tier society that might result.

Many Christians are concerned about the research stage in gene therapy and the possible suffering caused to animals. Yet others worry that gene therapy is just the start of what will become a slippery slope leading to designer babies being created. Some Christians question the amount of money being spent on research into rare conditions when there are so many other more common diseases and conditions that need research money.

Many Christians, however, think the benefits of somatic-cell therapy outweigh the risks and costs. How can a price be put on the life of a child? As with assisted conception, it is an extension of Jesus' healing ministry, a responsible use of God-given skills and an act of compassion.

Roman Catholics in particular are opposed to the creation of saviour siblings, and this is for several reasons: IVF is against Natural Law, spare embryos are created and wasted in the PGD procedure, and it exploits the resulting child, which is incapable of giving consent. Some Christians of other denominations are also opposed to it because it seems exploitative and can lead to problems if the treatment fails. Others, however, accept it, provided that the child is wanted for his or her own sake.

# Questions and activities

## Sample questions and answers

**1** Explain what is meant by a saviour sibling. (2 marks)

 A child conceived through IVF to be a genetically compatible match for a seriously ill brother or sister.

## 5

## Commentary

An accurate explanation of the term is needed for two marks.

**2** Give two reasons why some people might want to select the sex of their child. (2 marks)

They might want to avoid a sex-related genetic disorder. They might also have several boys and want to be sure that their next child is a girl.

## Commentary

One mark is given for each reason, so two short sentences are sufficient.

**3** Explain Christian attitudes to somatic-cell therapy. (6 marks)

Many Christians support this because it saves the life of someone who would otherwise die. God gave humans the skill to put nature right by correcting faulty genes, and he would want doctors to make good use of that skill. During his lifetime, Jesus healed many people, and gene therapy is a reflection of the compassion that he showed to people who were suffering. Not all Christians accept it, however. Some disagree with animals being used in any experimentation, since it causes them suffering; moreover, the animals did not consent to it, so it is exploitative. Others are concerned about a slippery slope from therapeutic genetic engineering to the creation of designer babies. There are also Christians who have no issues with the actual technique, but think that the money would be better spent in other ways, e.g. finding a vaccine for leprosy, rather than in researching what are very rare conditions.

## Commentary

Because this answer carries six marks, it is important to give a detailed response that covers a wide range of Christian opinion.

## Further questions

**1** Explain why some Christians accept the creation of saviour siblings. (2 marks)

**2** Explain why some Christians are against the creation of saviour siblings. (2 marks)

**3** 'People who want designer babies should be able to have them.' Do you agree? Give reasons for your answer, showing that you have thought about more than one point of view. Refer to Christian teachings in your answer. (6 marks)

## Class activities and homework

### Somatic-cell genetic engineering

In pairs, find out about the cases of Rhys Evans and Freddie. Go onto the website www.jeansforgenes.com. To find out about Rhys, and to watch a video about his treatment, click on *How Your Money Helps*. To find out about Freddie, go to the bottom of the home page and click on *Children's Stories*.

Find out about Steven Howarth, who was blind, by going onto the website www.timesonline.co.uk/tol/news/uk/health/article3828715.ece

Using your understanding of how gene therapy works and of cases where it has been used, create a poster encouraging people to give to the Jeans for Genes charity.

## Useful websites

www.cofe.anglican.org Click on *About the Church*, then *Social and Public Issues, Science & Medical Ethics* and *Genetics*.

www.ethicaldimension.org Click on *Embryo Research*, *Designer Babies* and *Saviour Siblings*.

www.cmf.org.uk Click on *Ethics and Issues*, *Stem Cells* and *Saviour Siblings*.

www.jeansforgenes.com

http://news.bbc.co.uk

http://learn.genetics.utah.edu

# Section 6

# Cloning

Cloning means creating a genetically identical copy of an organism. Since the creation of Dolly the sheep in 1997, artificial cloning of animals has become a reality. Scientists have now turned their attention to humans.

## Reproductive cloning

Some individual doctors in other countries have claimed success in **reproductive cloning**, but this has never been proved. In the UK, reproductive cloning is illegal.

## Therapeutic cloning

Some UK research establishments have been given licences to conduct research into **therapeutic cloning**. This type of cloning entails taking the nucleus out of an egg and replacing it with the nucleus from an adult human cell. The egg is then stimulated to become an embryo from which stem cells can be removed after six days. Most of the research carried out in this way is aimed at learning how to develop replacement tissues or organs for a whole variety of diseases and conditions. One piece of research involves using adult cells from people with motor neurone disease. In this case, cells are taken from the embryo for research at an earlier stage and the embryo is destroyed at six days.

One of the problems with therapeutic cloning is the shortage of human eggs, so in May 2008 a majority of British members of parliament voted to allow the use of **hybrid embryos** for research. As with the use of human embryos, licences would have to be obtained by research institutes and the embryos would have to be destroyed at 14 days.

**Key word**

**Hybrid embryos**
Embryos created by inserting human genetic material into empty cow's eggs

# General arguments for and against cloning

There are a number of arguments in support of cloning:

- Therapeutic cloning would save lives, show compassion and avoid the need for expensive anti-rejection drugs following organ transplants.
- Reproductive cloning is another form of compassionate fertility treatment.
- People have the right to choose how they reproduce.
- Cloning may assist the progress of evolution and it is wrong to stand in the way of medical and scientific progress.
- The use of hybrid embryos would remove the need for human eggs to be available for research.

There are, however, concerns about all types of cloning:

- It is unnatural. This would be particularly so with hybrid embryos.
- Many scientists doubt the real value of hybrid embryos in research and also claim that it is not necessary to use embryos at all. Research into the use of adult stem cells is just as likely to produce good results and this would not give rise to ethical issues.
- It took almost 300 nuclei and 30 cloned embryos to produce Dolly, and reproductive cloning could result in deformed foetuses and babies.

## 6

- Reproductive cloning would blur a person's unique identity and damage the structure of the family. Cloned children would simply be manufactured products.
- Instead of assisting human survival, cloning could reduce the human gene pool and humans might select themselves out of existence.

# Religious views on cloning

## Christianity

All Christians oppose any attempts at reproductive cloning as it is unnatural. Moreover, the desire some people have for a copy of themselves can be seen as idolatrous. It is exploitation of an embryo and the clone is just a commodity. Above all, cloning is 'playing God' in a way that could have disastrous results, psychologically and socially. The risks are enormous, as can be seen from all the unsuccessful attempts to produce a perfect animal clone. Even though Dolly was a success, she aged and died prematurely.

Christians are more divided over therapeutic cloning. The official Anglican view is that therapeutic cloning is an acceptable use of God-given intelligence and skills and an act of compassion, continuing Christ's healing work. So long as the legal cut-off point is observed, the embryo being experimented on is not human life in any meaningful sense.

Roman Catholics are totally opposed to therapeutic cloning because of their views on embryology. The recent Vatican document 'The Dignity of a Person' says both reproductive and embryonic stem-cell cloning risk dragging humanity into 'biological slavery'.

There is a great deal of unease among Christians of all denominations about the creation and use of hybrid embryos. Some Christians see the potential of any such development, but many are worried that boundaries will continue to be pushed back, and that we are on the edge of a slippery slope that will lead to our to treating embryos simply as research material. Cardinal Keith O'Brien, Scotland's most senior Catholic, denounced the idea of hybrid embryos as blasphemous, monstrous and 'playing God'.

# Questions and activities

## Sample questions and answers

**1** Explain why some Christians support research into cloning.

(3 marks)

Some Christians support research into therapeutic (stem-cell) cloning because, if it could be done, it would save many lives. Those who were treated would not fear their body's rejection of a new body part. Some Christians do not think that before 14 days an embryo is an individual person or can feel pain, and research is only allowed up to that point.

### Commentary

The command word 'explain' and the allocation of 3 marks mean that it is not enough to give a simple list. There needs to be some detail.

**2** Explain why some Christians oppose research into cloning.

(3 marks)

Some Christians oppose research into reproductive cloning. They see this as taking medical science too far and 'playing God'. Roman Catholics oppose all research into cloning, whatever its aims. They believe an embryo has full human rights from the point of conception, so to perform research on it and then destroy it is an act of killing.

### Commentary

The same points apply as given in the commentary to the previous answer.

**3** 'Medical scientists should be left to get on with their research without interference from religious believers.' Do you agree? Give reasons for your answer, showing that you have thought about more than one point of view. You should refer to Christian teachings in your answer.

(6 marks)

Medical research has led to some wonderful discoveries in the past few decades that have saved many lives and made life free of pain and disability for others. Why should people have to be infertile just because some people who can have children decide that medical scientists should not 'play God'? Those who work in medical research are responsible human beings and know where to draw the line. Many of them are religious believers anyway.

Nevertheless, I can see why many Christians are concerned. Medical scientists may have good intentions, but it is all too easy to get carried away and to want to push the boundaries that bit further. The possible consequences of unwise medical research are terrifying. Many people agree that God gave them their brains and their skills, but there are limits beyond which they should not go, and meddling with human life exceeds those limits. After all, God is the source of life.

I can see the dangers in such research, but I also think that it is not for Christians to set restrictions unless they are experts in medical issues. I'm sure that medical scientists would not want to tell the pope what to believe and to do. So, overall, I agree with the statement. I think the possible benefits for humans are too great to ignore, and I trust medical scientists to know where to stop.

## Commentary

This is an evaluation question that is well argued, examines different views and contains religious content.

## Further questions

**1** What are hybrid embryos? (1 mark)

**2** Why did some scientists think it was necessary to use hybrid embryos? (1 mark)

**3** 'Christians who believe that life is sacred should never support stem-cell research.' What do you think? Explain your opinion.

## Class activities and homework

## Radio phone-in on embryo research

Your teacher will assign the following roles: chairperson, medical scientist carrying out research into stem-cell cloning, a Roman Catholic priest, an Anglican priest who holds different views from the Roman Catholic position, the wife of a man paralysed from the neck down because of an accident. The rest of you will be able to phone in and ask questions of any of those people or make comments on what is said by them or by other listeners. Spend time thinking about the issue and what you might ask. Then hold the radio phone-in.

Write up a summary of the radio phone-in, stating those views that struck you as the most important and those that you most strongly agreed or disagreed with.

Go to the Genetic Science Learning Center website: http://learn.genetics.utah.edu. On this informative hands-on site you will learn all kinds of things about genetic engineering and cloning, and you can 'clone a mouse'. Make notes on points that you might use in essays.

## Useful websites

www.cofe.anglican.org. Click on *About the Church*, then on *Social and Public Issues*, *Science & Medical Ethics* and *Human Fertilsation & Embryology*.

www.ethicaldimension.org Click on *Embryo Research*.

www.cmf.org.uk Click on *Ethics & Issues*, then *Cloning*.

http://news.bbc.co.uk

http://learn.genetics.utah.edu

http://re-xs.ucsm.ac.uk Click on *Ethical & Moral Issues*, then on *Medical Ethics & Genetics*.

# Personal responsibility

# Sexual relationships

In the New Testament, Paul told the Christians of Corinth that, since their bodies were temples of the Holy Spirit, they should be respected and not abused. The way they treated their bodies should therefore reflect both personal responsibility and commitment in their relationships with others.

## Secular attitudes to same-sex relationships

Attitudes to sexuality and sexual relationships have changed considerably since the middle of the twentieth century. Changes in laws relating to **homosexuality** have meant that gay men and women should be able to 'come out' without fear, but there are still instances of violence against them. Gay couples are now more open about their relationships.

**Key word**

**Homosexuality**
Being sexually attracted to people of the same sex

The debate as to why some people have a homosexual orientation is still ongoing: some think the causes are genetic, others think in terms of environmental influences.

# Christian attitudes to same-sex relationships

Attitudes vary widely. Many Christians differentiate between inclination and practice. The Roman Catholic Church teaches that people with homosexual tendencies 'must be accepted with respect, compassion and sensitivity' (Catechism of the Catholic Church). There should be no discrimination against them. At the same time, the Catechism states that they must practise chastity because homosexuality goes against natural law.

In recent years the Anglican Church has been torn apart by disputes over whether practising homosexuals should be accepted as ordained priests or bishops. Some Anglicans take their stand on biblical teaching that homosexual tendencies and practices are sinful (Romans 1:26–27). Others claim that these teachings are outdated and that they referred to the promiscuous homosexual practices that were common in the ancient world and not to the loving same-sex relationships of today. The official stance is that, to set an example, Anglican clergy should not be practising homosexuals, but it is seen as a matter for individual conscience.

Matt Lucas and Kevin McGee. Registering a civil partnership allows gay couples to enjoy the same rights as married couples

Toby Melville/Reuters/Corbis

The Methodist Church in its 1993 Resolutions on Human Sexuality 'affirms and celebrates the participation and ministry of lesbians and gay men in the church'.

# Secular attitudes to heterosexual relationships

Safe **contraception** and abortion mean that unmarried people no longer fear sexual relationships leading to pregnancy. Attitudes to children born outside marriage have also changed, and the UK has the highest teenage pregnancy rate in Europe.

The media emphasise sex as something to be enjoyed and tend to assume that people are sexually active at a young age. Many teenage magazines focus on sexual issues, and sex is a prominent theme of many television programmes and films.

Nevertheless, the legal age of consent for sexual intercourse remains at 16 years. This is to prevent exploitation of and harm to young people.

## Key words

**Adultery**
A sexual relationship between two people, at least one of whom is married to someone else

**Casual sex**
Sex without commitment

**Cohabitation**
Where a couple live together and enjoy a sexual relationship without being married

**Contraception**
Use of any of a range of methods to prevent pregnancy

**Extra-marital sex**
A sexual relationship between two people who are not married to each other; they may be single or married to someone else

**Pre-marital sex**
Sexual intercourse before marriage

# Different types of extra-marital sexual relationships

It is important to distinguish between **extra-marital sex** engaged in by two single people (often referred to as **pre-marital sex**) and sex where at least one of the two people is married to someone else (**adultery**). With pre-marital sex, there is also another distinction that some religious believers make: recreational or **casual sex** (e.g. one-night stands) and sex within a relationship (e.g. where two people live together without being married). Living together without being married is known as **cohabitation**.

# Christian attitudes to heterosexual relationships

Sexuality is seen as one of God's most precious gifts. Genesis describes Adam's delight when Eve was created and the joy of their sexual relationship: 'The man and the woman were both naked, and they felt no shame.' (Genesis 2:25)

The Song of Solomon, also in the Old Testament, is a collection of explicit love poems: 'How beautiful your sandaled feet, O prince's daughter! Your graceful legs are like jewels, the work of a craftsman's hands.' (Song of Solomon 7:1)

After his conversion to Christianity, Paul travelled through Europe, telling anyone who would listen about Jesus. He made many converts and kept in touch with them, answering questions and giving moral and spiritual guidance in letters. In most of his letters he discussed sexual relationships, but this was a particular issue for the church community at Corinth. They asked him whether or not they should marry and his reply displayed a far more cautious attitude to sexual relationships than is seen in the Old Testament. This was partly because he saw clearly from the pagan environment in which he lived that uncontrolled sexuality could have terrible results. The Corinthians were notoriously promiscuous.

Paul also believed that the end of the world was imminent, and that Christians should be preparing for that instead of being distracted by sex. He told the Christians at Corinth to remain celibate but if their sexual urges were strong they should marry, for there was no shame in it. Above all, he also told them that their bodies were temples of the Holy Spirit. They should respect their bodies as they would a place of worship (1 Corinthians 6:18–20).

Throughout the history of the Church, **celibacy** has been valued. Roman Catholic priests are not allowed to marry and neither are monks and nuns (both Roman Catholic and Anglican). Some Christians choose celibacy as a way of showing their devotion to God.

For most Christians, however, sexual relationships are important. The official teaching of all denominations is that sex should be restricted to marriage. This is because marriage demands the commitment needed for the greatest enjoyment of sexual relationships. Marriage also provides a stable environment for rearing children, which the Roman Catholic Church claims is the primary purpose of sex. Christians in other denominations do not agree with this. They think that sexual pleasure is important in its own right, although they would probably agree that the best context for sex is marriage.

A movement to win teenagers back to traditional sexual values and promote **chastity** started in the USA in 1993. It was known as 'True Love Waits'. Teenagers, who may or may not be virgins, promise not to have sex before marriage, and they sign a card. Parents or supporters give the young person a ring, saying, 'Let this ring be a constant

## Key words

**Celibacy**
Not having a sexual relationship within or outside marriage, often as a result of a religious promise

**Chastity**
Having moral standards and restraint as regards sexual relations

Lydia Playfoot took her school to the High Court after she was banned from wearing her silver chastity ring to school

reminder to you to be sexually pure.' In 1996 the Silver Ring Thing movement was launched, and it has now become global.

However, many Christians recognise that society has changed and that the reasons given in the past for confining sex to marriage are no longer valid. These Christians accept loving and committed sexual relationships but do not approve of recreational or casual sex.

All Christians take seriously the seventh Commandment (for Roman Catholics, the sixth), 'Do not commit adultery,' and Jesus' teaching in Matthew 5:27–28 that the thinking and the desire behind adultery is as bad as the act itself. Adultery causes terrible hurt and a sense of betrayal. It is seen as a form of cheating and dishonesty. Once one partner has been unfaithful to the other, it is hard to build up trust again.

# Contraception

Many types of contraception are available, including:

- barrier methods such as the condom
- the coil (intra-uterine device)
- the pill
- the morning-after pill

Barrier methods and the pill prevent fertilisation. The coil and morning-after pill prevent implantation of the fertilised egg in the uterus. More permanent forms of contraception are vasectomy for men and tubal tie for women.

Most people use contraception because they do not want children at the time. Some, however, have a hereditary condition they do not want to pass on to children, or use condoms to avoid sexually transmitted infections (STIs).

There are other natural forms of family planning. The most common of these is the rhythm method, which follows the rhythm of the menstrual cycle and seeks to ensure that a woman has sexual intercourse when she is least fertile.

## The Christian viewpoint

Roman Catholics believe that the main purpose of sexual intercourse is to procreate (to conceive children). The official teaching is that all artificial forms of contraception are sinful. All interfere with God's purpose, and the coil and morning-after pill are forms of abortion. Fertility is a gift from God.

Natural methods are allowed, since these do not prevent the fulfilment of God's will. The Catechism of the Catholic Church recognises that parents may want to space the births of their children.

Some priests do not agree with the official teaching of the Church. They advise couples to act according to conscience. Some do not feel bound by the Church's teaching on contraception, since it was not given by the pope *ex cathedra* (i.e. with his full authority and infallibility).

Protestants see children as a precious gift from God, but they do not consider procreation to be the main purpose of sexual relationships. The decision of couples to use contraception is a valid use of free will. God created humans in his own image, giving them dominion over creation (Genesis 1:27). The decision not to have children or to space them out might be a responsible use of God-given autonomy.

Contraception should be used within marriage but Protestants also believe that if an unmarried couple intend to have a sexual relationship but cannot support a child, then the responsible thing is to use contraception. If someone is going to have casual sex, then it should be 'safe sex' (with a condom), to prevent the spread of STIs.

# Questions and activities

## Sample questions and answers

### 1 What is meant by chastity?                    (2 marks)

Chastity is exercising self-control and remaining sexually pure.

### Commentary

For two marks some development is needed, but there is no need to answer at length.

### 2 Name two types of contraception.                    (2 marks)

The pill, the condom.

### Commentary

There is no need to write a sentence. Accurate information is sufficient.

### 3 Explain Christian attitudes to the use of contraception.  (6 marks)

Many Christians view the use of contraception as a responsible act by a married couple who may not want children or who cannot afford to have more. It may be that one of the two carries a genetic disease but the couple do not wish to use IVF and discard affected embryos. Ideally contraception should be a matter for married couples, as Christians see marriage as the best environment for a sexual relationship. But if an unmarried couple are going to have a sexual relationship then it is better to use reliable contraception than to risk bringing an unwanted child into the world or having an abortion.

Roman Catholic teaching, however, opposes all forms of artificial contraception. Those who follow this teaching believe that every act of sexual intercourse should be open to God's gift of children. They believe that using contraception is an act of defiance against God, and they see the use of the coil or the morning-after pill as equivalent to abortion. There are, however, some individual Roman Catholics who believe that, in certain situations, using artificial forms of contraception as opposed to relying on natural family planning is the wise thing to do.

## Commentary

Because this is a 6-mark question, the answer needs to be detailed. The best way of achieving this is to look at both positive and negative attitudes to contraception.

## Further questions

**1** What in the UK is the legal age of consent for sexual intercourse? (1 mark)

**2** What is the difference between pre-marital sex and adultery? (1 mark)

**3** 'The teaching of the Christian Church on sex is outdated.'
What do you think? Explain your opinion. (3 marks)

**4** Explain different Christian attitudes towards homosexuality. (4 marks)

## Class activities and homework

### 'True love waits'

Or does it? In small groups, find out more about the True Love Waits and Silver Ring Thing organisations from the internet and say what you think about their views and the way they work. Report back to the rest of the class.

Look at the Caris website (www.carismag.co.uk) and in particular at what it has to say about relationships with the opposite sex. Compare it with other teenage magazines. Which approach do you think is more relevant to young teenagers?

Do you think contraception should be automatically and more easily available to those under the age of 16? Give reasons for your opinion.

## Useful websites

www.request.org.uk Click on *Issues*, then *A–Z of Issues* and *Sexuality*.
www.silverringthing.org.uk
www.carismag.co.uk

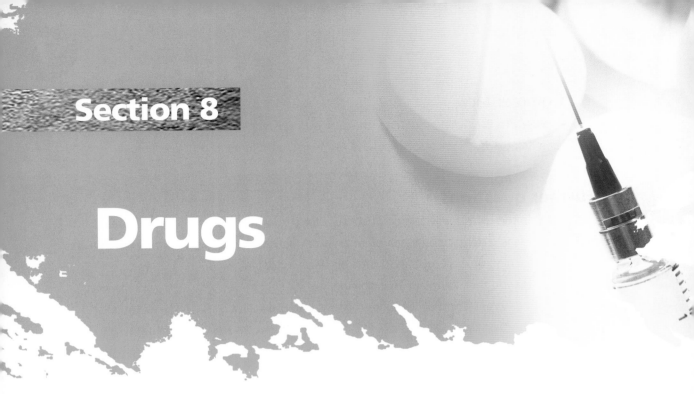

# Section 8

# Drugs

A drug is a natural or artificial substance that we take into the body and which has physical and/or emotional and mental effects. These effects may be beneficial or harmful, depending on the nature of the drug and the amount taken. Some drugs are legal, some are legal when taken on medical prescription, and others are illegal.

There are numerous reasons why people take drugs, some of which are:
- for medicinal/therapeutic benefit
- for social reasons
- to improve sporting performance
- peer pressure
- escapism

## Legal drugs

These are drugs which adults can buy freely, e.g. paracetamol. So long as the accompanying guidelines are followed, they are not harmful.

Caffeine is a drug taken by most people in everyday drinks and in chocolate. It is a stimulant and many people drink coffee to help them stay awake.

Tobacco and alcohol are much more controversial because there are serious health risks associated with both of these social drugs. Both are highly taxed.

## 8

Some people support even higher taxes, partly to discourage their use but also to fund research into associated health issues. Health services could then spend their existing budgets on treating those whose illnesses were not caused by these habits.

## Tobacco

Smoking is the biggest cause of preventable death in Britain, accounting for a high proportion of heart and respiratory diseases and cancers, which cost the NHS millions of pounds each year. If a pregnant woman smokes, she is likely to give birth to a child with health and development problems.

Non-smokers suffer the effects of **passive smoking**. As a result of breathing in other people's cigarette smoke they may suffer potentially fatal health problems.

In addition smoking pollutes the environment, creates litter and causes fires. In recent years there have been attempts to discourage smoking, and in the UK it is now banned in all enclosed public places.

> **Key word**
>
> **Passive smoking**
> When someone who does not smoke inhales smoke exhaled by someone who does

Those who choose to smoke complain that their rights are being infringed, and that nobody should tell them what they may or may not do. Some argue that the dangers have been exaggerated.

## Alcohol

Although alcohol causes fewer deaths per annum than smoking, it can be seen as a more serious problem because it is much more socially acceptable. Ninety per cent of adults drink, though the majority do so within reasonable limits. The increase in binge drinking has created major problems throughout Britain. Many underage teenagers get drunk on a regular basis. Drinking alcohol is seen as a 'cool' thing to do.

Alcohol is addictive and alcoholics may even steal from family members to pay for the next bottle. Ex-addicts know that just a sip of alcohol could trigger alcoholism again and it is a disease that kills. Alcohol consumption is a major cause of fatal illness and injury. It also contributes to domestic violence and homelessness.

Cannabis was reclassified as a class-B drug in January 2009

## Key words

**Gateway drug**
A soft drug that may lead someone on to use hard drugs

**Hard drugs**
Also known as class-A drugs; these cause the most damage and are often addictive

**Soft drugs**
Also known as class-B drugs; these are less harmful and less addictive than hard drugs, but are illegal and can cause serious problems

# Illegal drugs

It is illegal to supply or possess certain drugs, and people doing so are liable to prosecution. The penalties vary according to the drug's classification, which is in turn dependent on the dangers it poses. Class A drugs, often referred to as **hard drugs**, are the most dangerous. They can lead to permanent physical or psychological damage and even death. They are generally addictive. Heroin, cocaine, ecstasy and LSD are all class A drugs. Class B drugs, often referred to as **soft drugs**, may also cause serious physical or psychological harm and may be addictive. Barbiturates and amphetamines fall into this category. The government reclassified cannabis from class C to class B in January 2009, because research suggests it can lead to serious mental problems.

# Drug-taking in Britain

Britain has the most serious drugs problem in Europe. In many other countries, people taking drugs are referred for treatment instead of being punished. Many people would like to see that policy adopted here, or to see all drugs being legalised, to stop the activities of drug dealers. Others think legalising drugs would worsen the problem and encourage people to move from soft to hard drugs. Cannabis is often referred to as a **gateway drug**, i.e. a soft drug leading to hard drugs.

# Helping drug addicts

The treatment of drug addicts has several aims: reduction in drug abuse, improvement in physical, emotional and mental health, and rehabilitation. Individual and group therapy is important as addicts often have a range of psychological problems bound up with their addiction. There are some residential centres for those whose problems are especially severe. Treatment centres may be funded by the government and local authorities or else set up and funded by charities or privately run. Funding is a problem, but without sufficient money put into treatment, addicts are unlikely to be rehabilitated. The government has reported an increase in those entering drug-treatment programmes but at the same time there is a high drop-out rate. It has been suggested that those who are most likely to drop out before completion are the addicts who have been made to attend the programmes by the criminal justice system.

# Christian attitudes to legal drugs

Christians believe that, although human beings seem small and insignificant in relation to the vastness of creation, God has given them a dignity beyond price (Psalm 8:4–5). Jesus taught that, although God cares deeply for all creatures, humans are of more worth (Luke 12:6–7). The psalmist wrote: 'You created every part of me; you put me together in my mother's womb' (Psalm 139:13).

So Christians value both body and mind, and medicinal drugs should be used if necessary. The body is a temple of the Holy Spirit and is to be respected.

## Smoking

Most Christians discourage smoking because of the harm it causes. The money spent on cigarettes could be put to better use. Christians do not own their bodies but are called by God to be good stewards (Matthew 25:14–29), meaning that they should look after their bodies responsibly on behalf of God. Smoking is not wise stewardship.

## Alcohol

Attitudes to alcohol vary. Members of The Salvation Army are **teetotal** because they see the effects of alcohol in their work with homeless alcoholics. They don't want to set a bad example or cause problems for others (Romans 14:19–21).

**Key word**

**Teetotal**
Not drinking alcohol

Most other Christians think that drinking is permissible. The psalms describe wine as bringing joy to human life. Jesus drank, and the New Testament relates the story of him changing water into wine at a wedding. But drinking should be in moderation. The Old Testament warned that too much alcohol makes a person loud and foolish, and Christians are aware of the harm it can do. Many Christians work with alcoholics, in soup kitchens, drop-in centres or hostels. Some monastic communities have treatment centres.

## Christian attitudes to illegal drugs

All the main Christian denominations are opposed to the use of illegal drugs because of the harm they cause to individuals, families and society. Pope John Paul II referred to drug-taking as the new slavery as it takes away people's freedom. There are some Christians, however, who claim that cannabis causes less harm than socially acceptable drugs and should be legalised. Many Christians would agree to its use in the treatment of conditions such as multiple sclerosis.

Jackie Pullinger has devoted her life to helping drug addicts

Jesus said that, like a doctor, he was there for those who needed him (Mark 2:17), and taught his followers to show compassion. Christians therefore believe that drug addicts should be helped rather than denounced. Some Christians, like Jackie Pullinger, devote their lives to helping them. Others are involved in advice and drop-in centres and clinics. Ordinary Christians support such centres financially and with prayer.

# Questions and activities

## Sample questions and answers

### 1 What is a drug? (1 mark)

A drug is a substance that alters your mind and body.

#### Commentary

This 1-mark question requires a precise but brief answer.

### 2 Name two legal drugs. (2 marks)

Alcohol, caffeine.

#### Commentary

Two words are sufficient.

### 3 Explain why some Christians disagree with the use of alcohol. (4 marks)

Members of The Salvation Army and many Methodists are opposed to drinking alcohol. This is because of the harm it can cause. Drinking alcohol is not treating one's body as the temple of the Holy Spirit, as it may damage the liver and cause heart disease. It also kills off brain cells. People with a drink problem also affect other members of their family, e.g. money needed to buy essentials for the children may be spent on drink.

Harm is done to society generally, as employees take days off work to recover from hangovers. Driving after drinking is also the cause of many fatal accidents. All this shows a lack of love for one's neighbour.

#### Commentary

The allocation of 4 marks for this answer means that detailed explanation is needed. Do not just give a list.

# 4 Explain why many Christians accept the use of alcohol in moderation. (3 marks)

Most Christians do not oppose drinking alcohol, provided it is not to excess. Most Christian denominations use wine at the Eucharist, following what Jesus did at the Last Supper. Jesus himself drank wine, as did just about everyone in his day, and the writer of a letter to Timothy advised him to drink a little wine with his food as an aid to digestion (1 Timothy 5:23). This has recently been backed up by medical experts, who say that one glass of red wine a day is good for the body. Christians believe that it is important to look after the body, which is a temple of the Holy Spirit. Alcohol in moderation is seen as adding to the enjoyment of a meal or a social occasion.

## Commentary

Again, more than a list is required, although 3 marks are available.

## Further questions

**1** Name two illegal drugs. (2 marks)

**2** Explain two reasons why people take illegal drugs. (4 marks)

**3** 'Christians should not smoke tobacco.' What do you think?
Explain your opinion. (3 marks)

## Class activities and homework

### Alcohol

Your teacher will invite someone from Alcoholics Anonymous or from the police to talk about the problems associated with alcohol. Plan questions that you might ask.

### Illegal drugs

Using information from leaflets and books that your teacher will provide, create a table listing five illegal drugs and their effects.

Find out about the work with drug addicts that is carried out by the charity Yeldall Christian Centres (www.yeldall.org.uk)

## Useful websites

www.drugs.homeoffice.gov.uk

www.talktofrank.com

www.request.org.uk Click on *Issues*, then *Issues A–Z* and *Drugs*.

www.yeldall.org.uk

http://re-xs.ucsm.ac.uk Click on *Ethical & Moral Issues*, then *Health & Body*.

# Section 9

# Marriage

In Christianity, there is a strong emphasis on the ideas of community and responsibility for one another. It begins with the family, extends to the Christian community and from there it reaches out to the local neighbourhood, the nation and the world. This is reflected in the Bible, which starts with the family unit. A stable family life is the basis for a stable society.

A stable family life is the basis for a stable society

## 9

Marriage has changed dramatically in the last 30 years. The number of marriages registered each year has halved, and there are far fewer religious ceremonies. The average age for marriage has gone up to approximately 30, and increasing numbers are second or third marriages.

Marriage is a public declaration of commitment made by one person to another. People get married for all kinds of reasons. They want to share their lives with the one they love. They see marriage as the best way of developing companionship and of giving children a secure environment that will enable them to grow into well-adjusted adults. Some also think that it is the best environment for expressing sexuality.

Marriage is also a legal contract that gives each partner rights. A marriage is not valid unless it has been conducted by a legally authorised individual. This means that sometimes couples have two ceremonies, one civil and one religious.

# Christian attitudes to marriage

Most Christians see marriage as a **sacramental covenant** between two people that has been established by God. Jesus saw marriage as a lifelong commitment. Quoting Genesis, he said:

> At the beginning of creation God 'made them male and female. For this reason a man will leave his father and mother and be united to his wife, and the two will become one flesh.' So they are no longer two, but one. Therefore what God has joined together, let man not separate.
>
> (Mark 10:6–9)

In his letter to the Christians of Ephesus, Paul quoted the same Genesis passage. Self-giving love and respect were, he said, the central features of a marriage. He said that the relationship between husband and wife mirrored that between Christ and his Church. The man should love his wife as Christ self-sacrificially loved the Church.

**Key word**

**Sacramental covenant**
A sacred contract involving promises. It is a binding agreement in which God acts as witness

More controversially from a modern viewpoint, he said that wives were to submit to their husbands (Ephesians 5:22). Many Christians think that this attitude is out of date. Some fundamentalist Christians, however, believe that wives should obey their husbands, pointing out that Paul's teaching on the kind of love a man should show his wife would prevent him from behaving like a tyrant.

Christian marriages are not arranged, except where particular cultural influences are strong, and there are no racial or religious bans. Christians are expected to ensure that where cultures and/or faiths are different, there is mutual respect and tolerance. Roman Catholics especially are concerned about marriages where one partner is non-Catholic or non-Christian, and a priest would talk this situation over carefully with the couple. Most Christians also want their parents to approve, as family support is seen as a key factor in the success of a marriage.

Wedding preparation classes are organised by most Christian denominations to ensure that the couple are fully prepared for the difficulties that can occur during the marriage.

Most Christian marriage services follow a similar format. The Anglican ceremony states that marriage:

- was given by God at creation
- entails a process of growth that leads to physical, emotional and spiritual unity and companionship
- is intended to be lifelong
- enables the couple to experience the joy of sexual fulfilment and commitment
- provides a secure environment for bringing up children
- enriches and strengthens society

In the vows, each partner states the intention of remaining faithful until death, whatever the circumstances: 'for better, for worse, for richer, for poorer, in sickness and in health, to love and to cherish, till death us do part' (*Common Worship Services and Prayers for the Church of England: Marriage* © The Archbishop's Council, 2000).

These vows are made in God's presence and with him as witness. Rings, symbolising unending love and fidelity, are exchanged with the words: 'With my body I honour you, all that I am I give to you, and all that I have I share with you' (*idem*).

At this point, the priest declares that the two are married and joins together their right hands, quoting Jesus' command not to separate what has been joined by God. The couple are then blessed. The ceremony includes readings and prayers, and often hymns and a short sermon. In Roman Catholic and Anglican churches, Christians often have a **Nuptial Mass**.

**Key words**

**Nuptial Mass**
A service of Holy Communion held as part of the marriage ceremony

**Procreative sex**
Sex that has the possibility of conception

**Unitive sex**
The idea that sexual intercourse makes a couple one

The Roman Catholic ceremony also includes the statement that each partner is open to the gift of children, as a blessing from God. This ties in with the view that every sexual act should be both **unitive** and **procreative**.

Christians see marriage as a partnership of equals that has to be worked at if it is to succeed. Honesty, respect, commitment, faithfulness and loyalty are essential.

A wedding ring is a complete circle with no beginning or end, symbolising eternity

# Alternatives to marriage

People increasingly choose not to marry but instead to live together. They choose cohabitation for a number of reasons. Some do not want the commitment of marriage; they prefer a less binding relationship, believing that the lack of pressure will make it work better. Others cannot afford the wedding ceremony that they would like, and later discover that living together gives the level of security that they need. There are also those who claim that marriage is simply a legal contract and that they do not need a piece of paper or a ritual to demonstrate the level of their commitment to one another. They say that, as their rights are protected by law and there is no longer any stigma about being the child of unmarried parents, they can see no point in getting married.

Homosexual couples are unable to marry but they can legally register their partnerships in **civil partnership ceremonies**. This gives them rights similar to those of married couples. Official church teachings of the main Christian denominations forbid ceremonies of blessing for homosexual couples, such as exist in the Anglican Church on the remarriage of people who have been divorced, but some individual clergy flout the rulings and conduct blessings on civil partnerships.

**Key words**

**Civil partnership ceremonies**
Non-religious ceremonies that allow gay couples to legally register their partnerships

**Secular**
Not religious

# Why marriages fail

Almost all marriages go through rough patches. This is part of human nature. When major problems occur, **secular** and religious charities or groups may provide support to try to save the marriage or to prevent the break-up from being hostile. There are Christian marriage-counselling services, and many Christians would seek guidance and support from their priest or minister. For Roman Catholics and many Anglicans, taking the sacraments of the Eucharist and Reconciliation can help, and for all Christians prayer and reflection on relevant Bible passages is important.

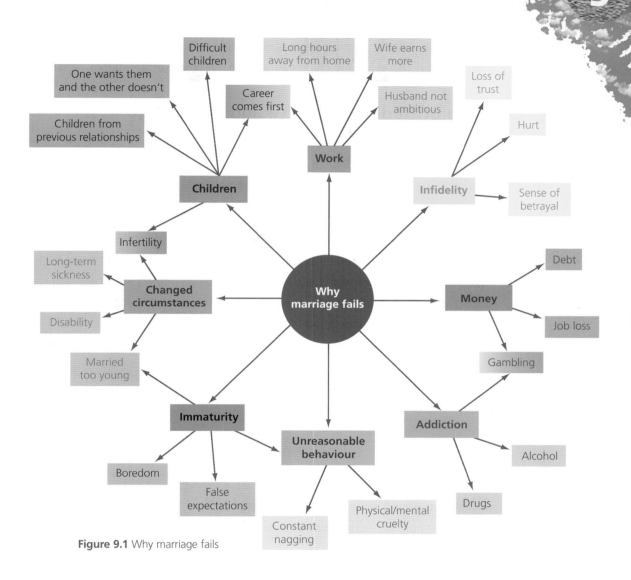

**Figure 9.1** Why marriage fails

# Divorce, annulment and remarriage

## The law

Divorce has been transformed over the past 50 years and it is now much easier to obtain one. Divorce is possible after a year of marriage, and one in three marriages ends this way. The sole ground for divorce in the UK is irretrievable breakdown of marriage. Remarriage is allowed without limit.

If it can be shown that the marriage was never valid in the first place, then it is annulled and there is no need for any divorce procedure. The partners are free to 'remarry'.

## Christian attitudes to divorce and remarriage

All Christians agree that marriage is intended to be lifelong, but there are differences of opinion about divorce and remarriage, partly because marriage is seen as a sacrament by Roman Catholics and some Anglicans, and partly because of differing approaches to the teaching of Jesus and Paul on divorce and remarriage.

According to Mark 10:2–12, Jesus said that divorce was never part of God's purpose. It was a concession to human weakness, and marriage was intended to be for life. Remarriage after divorce was effectively adultery (unless infidelity had been involved, according to Matthew 5:32). The passage from Mark raises a number of questions:

- Was Jesus making a law or stating an ideal?
- Was he trying to protect the status of women, who were made vulnerable by the divorce laws of his day?
- Were some or all of the verses on remarriage after divorce an addition by Mark for the Church in Rome, as women may not divorce men under Jewish law?
- Was the exception for infidelity in Matthew 5:32 an addition made to meet the needs of the Jewish Christian community for which that Gospel was written?

Paul said that couples should not divorce, save where a pagan partner wanted to divorce a husband or wife who had converted to Christianity. In that case, the Christian should agree to the divorce, but only for the sake of peace.

### Key words

**Eucharist**
One of the Christian sacraments, a service at which Christians eat bread and drink wine in remembrance of Jesus' death

**Reconciliation**
A sacrament that involves confessing your sins to a priest, who declares God's forgiveness

## Roman Catholics

Marriage is a **sacrament**. The vows cannot be dissolved because they are made in the name of God. Jesus was laying down a law for Christians to follow. The Roman Catholic Church does not recognise remarriage after divorce and many priests will not allow those who do remarry to receive Holy Communion. Those with marital problems should seek help from their families and friends, a marriage counsellor or priest. They should also seek help from the Bible, prayer and the sacraments, especially the **Eucharist** and **Reconciliation**.

A marriage can be ended by an **annulment** if it can be shown never to have been a true marriage. The partners are free to 'remarry'. Grounds for an annulment are if one of the partners:

- was forced into the marriage
- suffered from mental problems at the time
- did not intend to keep the vows
- was not baptised at the time of marriage

## Most Protestant denominations (e.g. Methodists and Baptists)

Although they take the marriage vows seriously, Protestants believe that:

- Humans are not perfect and sometimes divorce is necessary or the best course of action to take.
- Jesus was always willing to forgive and offer people a fresh start.
- Jesus' teaching on marriage was an ideal rather than a law.

Remarriage in church is permissible providing that the vows are taken seriously.

## Anglicans

Marriage is a sacrament and vows made in the presence of God are meant to be kept. An official statement acknowledges that there are situations when divorce and remarriage in church are acceptable, but in practice attitudes vary from church to church.

Some priests adopt the Roman Catholic view and do not see remarriage as valid. Others believe that divorce is sometimes the best option. However, since in their view marriage vows can be made only once, they do not allow remarriage in church. Instead, they may hold a service of marriage blessing after a civil ceremony. When Prince Charles married Camilla Parker Bowles in 2005, they had a civil ceremony at the Guildhall in Windsor, followed by a service of marriage blessing in St George's Chapel, Windsor Castle.

Some priests accept divorce, recognising that people make mistakes. They point to the example of Jesus, who was always willing to give people a second chance. They think that Jesus' teaching about divorce and remarriage was an ideal rather than a rule and accept that second marriages can be better than the first. They are willing to let couples remarry in church providing they take the vows seriously.

# The importance of family and the elderly

Commitment and responsibility are at the heart of family life. Parents are expected to give their children the love, security and Christian upbringing they will need throughout life. The Catechism of the Catholic Church states: 'Parents have the first responsibility for the education of their children in the faith, prayer and all the virtues. They have the duty to provide as far as possible for the physical and spiritual needs of their children.'

Children have the duty to honour and respect their parents, as stated in the fourth Commandment, and this extends throughout their lives. Christians believe that they should care for elderly relatives in whatever way is appropriate. Grandparents also have an important role to play in family life.

# Questions and activities

## Sample questions and answers

**1** What is meant by a civil marriage ceremony?                    (1 mark)

It is a non-religious wedding ceremony.

### Commentary
This is only worth 1 mark, so a short answer is sufficient.

**2** Explain the meaning and purpose of marriage for Christians.                    (5 marks)

Many Christians see marriage as a sacrament. This means it is a ceremony that carries God's special blessing. The bride and groom make a covenant with one another in the presence of God and the Church community. They make vows that they will stay together for life through thick and thin, and that they will cherish one another. There are three important purposes that marriage fulfils. The man and woman are companions, sharing good and bad experiences together. Their sexual lives are enriched through lovemaking, which is carried out only with each other. They work together to make their home a stable, secure and loving environment in which to bring up children. At the heart of their marriage are mutual love and respect for each other. The everlasting nature of their love is symbolised in the marriage service with the exchange of rings.

## Commentary

The allocation of 5 marks means that a detailed answer is required. This sample answer explains both the meaning of marriage and its purposes, as set out in the Anglican marriage service, and a number of developed points are made.

**3** 'Marriage is totally pointless in our modern world.' Do you agree? Give reasons for your answer, showing that you have thought about more than one point of view. You should refer to Christian teaching in your answer. (6 marks)

So many marriages break up nowadays that marriage does not seem to have any real point. The vows people make seem meaningless. Because people live longer now, the old idea of a lifelong loving relationship just isn't realistic. People change, situations change, and so it is hard for the love to last. Few people have any religious commitments now, so the whole idea of marriage as blessed by God and of making sacred promises is alien. In the past, people were shocked if you lived together and children born out of marriage were looked down on. All that has changed, so it really doesn't matter whether or not you are married.

On the other hand, many couples still choose to marry one another. Living together is just not the same. You don't make a public commitment when you move in with someone. You just move in! It's far too easy to leave if you are cohabiting. If they are married, people might think twice before getting divorced. This means that their children have a better chance of a stable home with two parents. A secure childhood means a secure adult. Although most people today are not practising Christians, they may want to promise to be faithful until death and to share everything. They want God's blessing as they start out on a new life together.

Overall, I think there is a point to marriage. Many people want to marry. They want it to last and if they have the support of their family and friends, the likelihood is that it will. Yes, one in three marriages breaks down. That means that two in three don't!

## Commentary

It would be easy to answer a question like this without any reference to religious views, but this is a Religious Studies exam so they must be included. You do not have to give only religious views, nor do you have to be a Christian yourself. You simply have to show how religious beliefs and teachings could support a particular view. You may wish to comment on the strengths or weaknesses of the religious arguments, and this would certainly help you towards gaining full marks. It does not matter whether the examiner agrees with you or not. All the examiner is looking for is your ability to evaluate two points of view and to see how Christian teachings might be relevant. This answer gives both viewpoints in some detail and ends with a brief conclusion that takes further the argument in support of marriage.

## Further questions

**1** What do Roman Catholics mean when they say that the main purpose of sexual intercourse is procreative? (1 mark)

**2** Explain some reasons why marriages fail. (3 marks)

**3** Do you think couples should stay together for the sake of their children? Give reasons for your answer. (4 marks)

**4** 'Couples who have made promises to God and then broken them should not be allowed to remarry in a church.' Give reasons for your answer, showing that you have thought about more than one point of view. (6 marks)

## Class activities and homework

### Finding out from the experts

Your teacher will invite a number of adults into the classroom, who will be prepared to answer questions relating to sex, marriage and divorce. One is likely to be the local priest/vicar. It may be possible to invite a marriage counsellor or legal expert. Bring your questions to the lesson.

Find out what is involved in getting a divorce from one of the websites that deals with this. Then write an answer to the following: 'Divorce is far too easy. Couples should have to work harder at making their marriages work.' Do you agree? Give reasons for your answer, showing that you have thought about more than one point of view. Refer to Christian teachings in your answer.

## Ten commandments for marriage

Draw up a list of your own ten commandments for marriage. Put them up on display and discuss in groups which commandments you think are the most important.

Choose any television soap and watch five episodes. Study the relationships between couples and note how they develop. Do you think their relationships could be improved and, if so, how? Do you think there is a future for them? Are the couples honest with one another? Do they love each other or are their relationships built on lust or exploitation?

## Useful websites

www.request.org.uk Click on *Issues*, then *A–Z of Issues* and *Divorce*, *Marriage* and *Sexuality*.

http://re-xs.ucsm.ac.uk Click on *World Religions*, then *Rites of Passage* and *Marriage*.

# Prejudice and discrimination

Old Testament laws and New Testament teachings alike stress the importance of commitment and **responsibility**. The Bible teaches that all people, irrespective of gender, race, culture, etc, are made in the image of God. They are all equal in God's eyes and should be treated justly.

## What are prejudice and discrimination?

**Prejudice** means having negative opinions about others without any sound reasons. It is literally 'pre-judging'.

**Discrimination** is the unfair treatment of others on the basis of prejudice. Generally, discrimination is negative — discriminating against someone. It can, however, be positive — discriminating in favour of someone. For example, positive discrimination has been applied by some British universities. They favour students from deprived backgrounds or under-achieving schools over those from independent schools.

**Key words**

**Discrimination**
Putting prejudice into action

**Prejudice**
An irrational opinion about an individual or group

**Responsibility**
The duty that humans have because of the power they exercise

# Causes of prejudice and discrimination

There are many reasons for prejudice and discrimination but the main one is ignorance. Lack of knowledge and understanding can easily lead to:

- **fear** through feeling threatened in some way
- **stereotyping** — thinking that everyone in a group has certain qualities (e.g. all football fans are hooligans)
- **scapegoating** — blaming certain groups for what is wrong in society

# Discrimination and the law

Although most forms of discrimination are illegal, it is still a problem in British society. The law might not give adequate protection if:

- the discrimination is subtle
- there are no witnesses
- witnesses are reluctant to give evidence, either because they do not want to be involved or because they fear some kind of backlash
- the discrimination is not reported because the victim is afraid of the offender seeking revenge
- the victim is not as articulate as the discriminator if the case comes to court or tribunal

## Key words

**British National Party (BNP)**
A far-right political party in the UK

**Scapegoating**
Blaming an innocent individual or group for something that is wrong

**Stereotyping**
Creating an oversimplified image of an individual or group, usually by assuming that all members of the group are the same

The law cannot dictate how people think. It cannot control prejudice, which can easily lead to discrimination. Some people are brainwashed by the prejudice of others (e.g. parents or the media) into believing that the law should be broken. Extremist nationalist groups such as the **British National Party (BNP)** have been accused of encouraging prejudice and whipping it up into hatred.

# Racial and colour discrimination

Black people and other ethnic minority groups are more likely to be victims of discrimination than white people. It may take a number of forms:

- verbal abuse such as name-calling
- physical attacks
- damage to property
- problems in finding jobs or being promoted

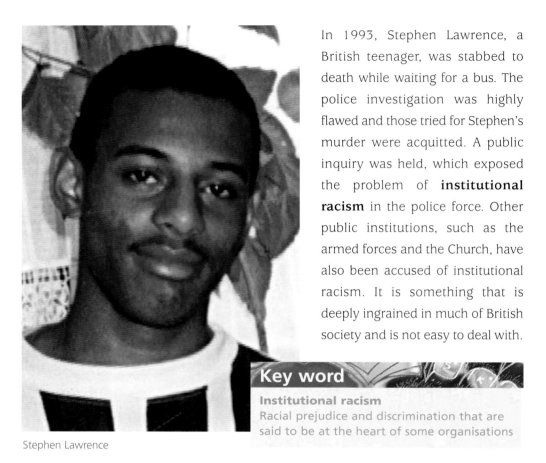

Stephen Lawrence

In 1993, Stephen Lawrence, a British teenager, was stabbed to death while waiting for a bus. The police investigation was highly flawed and those tried for Stephen's murder were acquitted. A public inquiry was held, which exposed the problem of **institutional racism** in the police force. Other public institutions, such as the armed forces and the Church, have also been accused of institutional racism. It is something that is deeply ingrained in much of British society and is not easy to deal with.

> **Key word**
>
> **Institutional racism**
> Racial prejudice and discrimination that are said to be at the heart of some organisations

## Laws relating to racial discrimination

The 1976 Race Relations Act bans discrimination on the grounds of racial origins in all key areas of life:

- housing
- education
- employment
- welfare

It is illegal to say or do anything that might stir up racial hatred.

The Commission for Racial Equality (now the Equality and Human Rights Commission) was set up to monitor and deal with racial discrimination. In 2000, further laws were passed to prevent racial discrimination in national and local government, hospitals and schools.

# Religious discrimination

Laws passed in 2003 and 2006 have extended existing laws to make discrimination on the grounds of religious beliefs or no religious beliefs illegal. This has been made necessary in recent years because of people's reaction to the threat of terrorism. **Islamophobia** in particular has become a major concern: the 9/11 attack on the Twin Towers in New York and the 7/7 bombings in London led some people to assume that all Muslims were terrorists. Some mosques were set alight and a number of those thought to be Muslim were beaten up. Other religious groups, too, are discriminated against because of their religious beliefs and practices. **Anti-semitism** continues to be a major problem.

## Key words

**Anti-semitism**
Hatred of Jews that expresses itself in discrimination

**Islamophobia**
Irrational fear of Muslims that leads to discrimination

**Suffragette movement**
A reform movement in the early twentieth century that aimed to secure the right for women to vote

# Gender discrimination

Victims of gender discrimination are usually women. Until the beginning of the twentieth century, women in the UK were regarded as the property of their fathers or husbands. Attitudes began to change during the First World War, when women had to do 'men's work'. The **Suffragette movement** led to women being given the right to vote.

However, for several decades after gaining the right to vote, women were expected to stop working when they got married. It was only towards the end of the twentieth century that it became the norm for women to continue working after getting married and having children. Even then, some jobs were still seen as more suitable for men, but women can increasingly be found in what were traditionally male-dominated careers, such as engineering and the sciences.

Nevertheless, many women are still not paid as well as men and it may not be easy for them to get the most senior jobs. When they do, they often face resentment and harassment. Many women work part-time so that they can spend more time with their children, but by doing so they are especially vulnerable to discrimination.

Illustrated London News

Suffragettes were prepared to break the law to gain the right for women to vote

## Laws relating to gender discrimination

The Equal Pay Act 1970 made it illegal for employers to discriminate between men and women in terms of their pay or conditions when they are doing the same or similar work. The Sex Discrimination Act 1975 made it unlawful to discriminate on the grounds of gender in:

- employment
- housing, goods, facilities and services
- education
- advertising

The Equal Opportunities Commission (now the Equality and Human Rights Commission) was set up to monitor and deal with gender discrimination.

# Disability discrimination

In the past, many disabled people were excluded from everyday activities. Those in wheelchairs often could not access public transport, shops, restaurants and cinemas. The needs of blind and deaf people were not met in the way information was given out. Disability sports such as the Paralympics were given little media coverage.

Much has changed for the better in recent years, but there is still underlying prejudice against disabled people that can lead to discrimination. It is often wrongly assumed that a disabled person is incapable of enjoying or contributing to life as much as someone without a disability.

## Laws relating to disability discrimination

The Disability Discrimination Act 1995 made it unlawful to discriminate on the grounds of disability in:

- employment
- provision of goods and services
- education

Because of the time and costs involved in carrying out the requirements of this Act (e.g. getting planning permission and making alterations to buildings), a long phasing-in period was allowed.

A more recent law has been passed to ensure that blind and deaf people have full access to information. For example, on trains both visual and auditory information is given about the journey.

# Christian attitudes to prejudice and discrimination

The following principles are central to Christian views on prejudice and discrimination:

- equality, which means that all human beings are of equal importance and value, and should be treated the same
- justice, which means that all human beings have the same rights to fair and equal treatment

In the past, many white Christians were guilty of discrimination, but now all Christians agree that it is sinful. The Catechism of the Catholic Church expresses the Christian position clearly: 'Every form of social or cultural discrimination in fundamental personal rights on the grounds of sex, race, colour, social conditions, language or religion must be curbed and eradicated as incompatible with God's design.'

Christians look to the example of Jesus, who was frequently rebuked for his friendship with outcasts. He was prepared to mix with and heal non-Jews, who were seen as unclean. He told a parable in which a Samaritan, whose people had long been bitter enemies of the Jews, was a hero.

Perhaps the most famous statement on equality comes from Paul: 'There is neither Jew nor Greek, slave nor free, male nor female, for you are all one in Christ Jesus' (Galatians 3:28).

On another occasion, Paul said, 'From one man he made every nation of men, that they should inhabit the whole earth...' (Acts 17:26).

Unfortunately, Christianity also has a history of discrimination against women. In the early centuries of the Church, a Church council decided by a majority of one

John Sentamu is the first black archbishop in the UK

that women were human beings! For centuries women were seen as just house-keepers and child-bearers. Throughout history, the Church has also had influential female role models such as Hildegard of Bingen, Catherine of Siena and Mother Julian of Norwich. In 1944 Li Tim-Oi was the first female priest to be ordained in the Anglican Church. She took on the role in Macao (a Portuguese territory on the coast of China) when priests could not travel there from Japanese-occupied territory during the Second World War. Once the war was over, she stopped working as a priest until the 1980s. She is now regarded as one of the great Christian women of the twentieth century.

Protestant churches have long had women ministers, and in 1994, the first women were ordained as priests in the Church of England. Many churches will not accept women priests, and there is a big debate about whether women should be bishops. The Roman Catholic Church ordains only men. It claims that this is not discrimination — women have a different role to play. Table 10.1 outlines some of the arguments in support of and against women priests.

**Table 10.1** Arguments for and against women priests

| Arguments against women priests | Arguments for women priests |
| --- | --- |
| Jesus chose only men as his disciples | Jesus did not choose women as his disciples because of the culture at the time |
| Some of Paul's teaching states that women are not to lead worship | In other passages Paul accepts women as having authority. In any case, society has changed since then |
| Having women priests has led to disunity in the Anglican Church. It would have been better to wait for a while | Sometimes a stand has to be made. Should Christians have waited until everyone agreed before they abolished slavery? |
| Men and women are essentially different | Women have a unique contribution to make |

# Martin Luther King Jr (1929–68)

Until the mid-twentieth century, black Americans were educated separately from whites and were not allowed access to the same facilities. Few had the right to vote.

Thanks to the **civil rights movement** and **Black Power** groups, by 1965 black Americans were given the same status as white Americans.

Martin Luther King Jr was perhaps the most important leader of the civil rights movement. He was inspired by the teachings of Mahatma Gandhi. During his time as a Baptist minister in Montgomery, Alabama, the civil rights movement was born. A black woman, Rosa Parks, was arrested in 1955 because she refused to give up her seat on a bus to a white man. This led to a bus boycott led by King, which continued despite intimidation until the law was changed.

Over a period of 10 years, a series of non-violent protest marches and sit-ins took place. These continued despite the violent backlash from the **Ku Klux Klan (KKK)** and other racists. In a march on Washington in 1963, King gave his famous 'I have a dream' speech in which he stated his vision of an America where his children would be judged by their characters rather than the colour of their skin. In 1964, King was awarded the Nobel peace prize, and the following year black people were given the vote.

Throughout the campaign, King stuck to a policy of non-violence, even though he was harassed by whites and verbally abused by blacks who thought he was weak. He spoke about the evil of violence being overcome by the power of love. In 1968, he was assassinated.

Although there is still deep-seated prejudice, the first black American president was elected in 2008, 40 years after King's assassination. Those who shared Martin Luther King's painful struggle for civil rights had cause for celebration.

## Key words

**Apartheid**
The policy of racial segregation and discrimination enforced by the white minority governments of South Africa

**Black Power**
A political movement among African Americans in the USA, which emphasised racial pride and promoted black interests

**Civil rights movement**
A movement that sought to gain justice for black people in the USA by non-violent means

**Ku Klux Klan (KKK)**
A white racist group in the USA

# Nelson Mandela and Desmond Tutu

From 1948 until 1994, the South African government's policy of **apartheid** meant that the black majority had no rights at all. They were forcibly relocated to townships outside the cities and had little access to proper education, health services and leisure facilities. International pressure in the form of **sanctions** and isolation eventually forced change, and now all citizens have equal rights whatever their racial origins. Problems still exist, however, and the crime rate is high partly because black poverty has not been eradicated.

During the terrible years of apartheid, two men came to different conclusions about the use of violence to change the system.

Nelson Mandela was brought up as a Methodist and trained as a lawyer. He joined the **African National Congress (ANC)** and tried in vain to achieve a change in the government's attitude by peaceful means. Eventually, he decided that violence was justified as the only way to destroy the evil system of apartheid, and in 1963 he was sentenced to life imprisonment for his activities.

He was released in 1990 by President F. W. de Klerk, who realised that the system had to change if South Africa was to survive politically and economically. Apartheid was dismantled and, in 1994, Mandela became the first democratically elected president. He set about achieving his vision of South Africa as a 'rainbow people', created the **Truth and Reconciliation Commission** as a way of healing wounds, and ended his country's isolation from the rest of the world.

Desmond Tutu trained to become a priest. After his ordination he studied further at King's College in London, eventually returning to South Africa as a lecturer. He was made a bishop and then an archbishop, using his position of authority to campaign against apartheid. Despite experiencing harassment from the government, he never changed his views on non-violence. He refused to use the methods of his opponents, and in 1984 he was awarded the Nobel peace prize. After the overthrow of apartheid, he was put in charge of the Truth and Reconciliation Commission.

## Key words

**African National Congress (ANC)**
A political party that was formed to increase the rights of black people in South Africa

**Sanctions**
Refusing to trade with a country or to supply what it needs

**Truth and Reconciliation Commission**
A body that investigated the crimes committed by both black and white people during the apartheid era, in the hope of getting people to face up to what they had done and to seek and receive forgiveness from their victims

# Questions and activities

## Sample questions and answers

**1** Explain, giving examples, the difference between prejudice and discrimination.                    (3 marks)

Prejudice means having opinions about someone without good reason, e.g. someone might think all blonde women are unintelligent. Discrimination is when prejudice is acted upon, e.g. if someone refuses to give a blonde woman a job, even though she is the best qualified of all the applicants, because of the belief stated above.

## Commentary

This question occurs quite frequently. It is essential that you know the difference between prejudice and discrimination.

**2** Explain some of the reasons for prejudice.          (4 marks)

The main cause of prejudice is ignorance. Some people do not understand why others behave in a certain way or dress in particular clothes. This sometimes makes them afraid. A man could hear a joke about women being bad drivers and, a short time afterwards, a woman drives into the back of his car. He thinks 'Typical woman' because he has been influenced by the views of others. That, together with his single bad experience, leads him to accept this stereotype of women.

## Commentary

This answer contains several reasons, with some discussion of them: ignorance, fear, influence of others, bad experience and stereotyping.

**3** How might a Christian try to stop discrimination?          (4 marks)

If the person is in a position of authority, he or she could use that position to influence others. For example, a priest could preach sermons against it. Even better, the pope could write an encyclical instructing all Roman Catholics not to discriminate against others. MPs can vote for laws that will prevent discrimination, and they can listen to and help anyone in their constituency who is a victim of it. Ordinary Christians can refuse to be part of any bullying or verbal abuse. They can make it clear that racist or sexist jokes are not funny. Above all, they can follow the example of Jesus and treat everyone with respect and kindness.

## Commentary

Because the question is worth 4 marks, both variety and development are needed. One way of achieving this is to approach the question from two different angles: an influential person and an ordinary religious believer. This enables good development to be made.

**4** Explain how one famous Christian has reflected Christian beliefs and teachings in his or her struggle against prejudice and discrimination. (4 marks)

Most of Martin Luther King Jr's adult life was devoted to the struggle for civil rights in the USA. Although he had a much better education than most black people of his day and could have led a comfortable life, he was willing to face persecution, harassment and imprisonment for what he believed in. He finally paid with his life, following Jesus' example of self-sacrificial love. In his vision of a USA where all people would be treated the same regardless of their colour, he reflected the teaching of Paul that racial differences are unimportant to God and the belief that all humans are children of God. His refusal to use violence followed Jesus' teaching about turning the other cheek. Like Paul, he said that the way to overcome evil was to respond positively with good.

## Commentary

You are required to know how religious beliefs have influenced the life of one well-known Christian. The example given here is of Martin Luther King Jr. It is important to write about more than just the person's life. You need to refer to specific Christian teaching and show how that influenced his or her actions.

## Further questions

**1** Give two types of discrimination. (2 marks)

**2** Explain Christian beliefs and teachings about prejudice and discrimination.

(4 marks)

**3** 'Not having women priests is a form of discrimination.' Do you agree? Give reasons for your answer, showing that you have thought about more than one point of view. (6 marks)

## Class activities and homework

### Types of prejudice

This section looks at three types of discrimination: race, gender and disability. Your teacher will divide the class into small groups and give each group one of these types of discrimination to research in greater depth. Find out how the law deals with it, discuss why it is a problem and consider what measures could be taken to prevent it. Put together a short presentation to give to the rest of the class.

Find out about the work of a Christian organisation that campaigns against discrimination. Present your findings in a format that will be useful for your revision.

Find out more about and make notes on the life of Li Tim-Oi and the work of the Li Tim-Oi Foundation.

### Campaigning against discrimination

Watch a film or documentary about Martin Luther King Jr, Nelson Mandela, Desmond Tutu, the American civil rights movement or apartheid.

Talk to someone at Citizens Advice about the kind of advice and support that are available to victims of discrimination.

Explore www.britkid.org to find out about daily life from the perspectives of teenagers of different races and religions.

## Useful websites

www.anc.org.za Click on *Site Index*, then *ANC Sites* and *The 'Mandela Page'*.

www.bbc.co.uk Type *Desmond Tutu* into the search engine for an audio interview and other web pages about him. Type *Martin Luther King* into the search engine for web pages about him.

www.britkid.org

www.litim-oi.org

www.request.org.uk Click on *Main Site*, then *History* and *20th and 21st Centuries* for information about Martin Luther King.

www.theforgivenessproject.com

# Global concerns

# Section 11

# The environment

Key Christian principles relating to global concerns, whether environmental or world poverty issues, are:

- **Stewardship**. This is the recognition that humans do not own the world but are entrusted by God with caring for it on his behalf. It entails using the world's resources in a way that does not exclude those in developing countries.

- **Justice**. This means fair treatment. Because humans are in a position of power, they have a duty to conserve the world and everything in it; those of us in the developed world are in an especially powerful position and have a duty towards people in developing countries.

- **Respect for life**. This is the recognition that everything and everyone in the world is God's creation and should be treated appropriately.

**Key words**

**Justice**
Treating everyone fairly and equally

**Respect for life**
Recognising that every living being has value

**Stewardship**
The idea that humans do not own the world but should look after it responsibly on behalf of God

# Environmental problems

Environmental problems are a big issue today. Some, such as drought, were known to our ancestors but are now experienced more frequently. Others are new problems.

Global warming is intensifying droughts

- Acid rain affects water in lakes, streams and soil. In Scandinavia, for instance, many lakes are unable to support fish, and some of this is due to wind-borne pollution from heavily industrialised countries like Britain. Contaminated water and food may be partial causes of respiratory and digestive disorders in humans. Trees are affected, and in the UK well over 60% of trees have suffered damage to their leaves or loss of needles. Some of the most beautiful buildings in Europe are also under threat from acid rain.
- Smog harms vegetation and humans.
- Rivers and lakes are polluted by agricultural, domestic and industrial waste. This kills marine life, and is a cause of cancer and birth defects in humans. In some parts of the world, major rivers are little more than open sewers.
- The sea becomes polluted from oil slicks, the dumping of industrial and domestic waste, and acid rain. This leads to toxic algae that kill marine life and contaminate seafood, pollute beaches and damage wildlife.

- Toxic waste is buried in deep holes or with domestic rubbish in landfill sites, which may cause health problems for those who live nearby.
- Pesticides and fertilisers kill wildlife and contaminate drinking water and human breast milk.
- An increase in the greenhouse gases that we produce is leading to global warming. This may result in flooding and the erosion of coastlines and low-lying coastal areas, as well as more severe droughts, storms and hurricanes. There may be an increase in the number and size of deserts.
- Thinning of the ozone layer may damage all forms of life.
- Over-fishing, hunting and the destruction of the rainforests are leading to the extinction of some species. There are fears that certain species of plants and animals that have never been discovered will vanish. Destruction of the rainforest is also contributing to climate change.

Unusually severe rainfall in one day in July 2007 led to flooding in many parts of southern England, including Oxford

# What can be done?

Some of the proposed solutions are so far-reaching and costly that they can only be achieved by international cooperation. However, not all nations wish to be involved. Some countries, e.g. the USA, refused to sign up to the **Kyoto Treaty** of 1997. President Obama, however, has stated that he wishes to see a dramatic cut in the USA's carbon emissions.

**Key word**

**Kyoto Treaty**
An international agreement to cut back on carbon emissions and deal with environmental problems

The EU has made an attempt to conserve fish stocks in the North Sea by the introduction of quotas. This is not popular with communities that depend on fishing for a living, and many fishing fleets have gone out of business.

Britain is slowly getting to grips with these issues. Recycling is becoming a feature of everyday life, with regular collections of glass, plastic and paper. CCTV cameras are being set up to prevent fly-tipping, and industries that pollute the atmosphere or rivers with their waste are being prosecuted and fined. Several cities are proposing to follow London in introducing a congestion charge, to keep cars out of the city centre. Car manufacturers are cutting down vehicle emissions. Improved public transport and the provision of cycle lanes help to reduce car traffic. Some consideration is being given to the use of renewable and natural energy sources. For instance, in Sweden 50% of domestic waste is incinerated to heat homes. Tree planting and reforestation are being encouraged in order to conserve wildlife.

The Green Party is a political party that focuses on environmental issues. Environmental pressure groups such as Greenpeace and Friends of the Earth educate the public and encourage people to become more 'green'.

Individuals, whether Christians or not, can contribute in a number of ways, as shown in Figure 11.1.

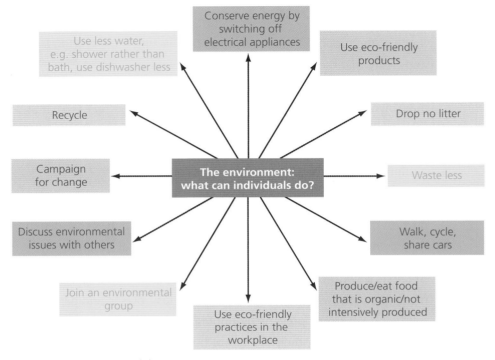

**Figure 11.1** Individuals and the environment

# Christian attitudes to the environment

The first two chapters of the Bible, Genesis 1 and 2, contain stories relating to the creation of the universe. They make a number of important points:

- God created everything.
- God created order out of chaos.
- Everything that he created was good, i.e. had its own integral value and fulfilled God's special purpose for it.
- Human beings were created with the capacity for a unique relationship with God, and they were in a position of authority.

In the past, Genesis 1 and 2 were not interpreted with sufficient care. It was believed they meant that God created everything with humans in mind. The words 'fill the earth and subdue it' (Genesis 1:28) were understood in terms of domination rather than responsible stewardship. Most Christians now believe that Earth and the whole of the universe have intrinsic value. They see it as their duty to conserve the planet for future generations. They recognise that they have great power over the world and its creatures, but that this power must be used responsibly. Humans do not own the planet; it is on loan and they have the sacred duty of caring for it on behalf of God. He created the universe so it should be treated with respect. The idea of the sanctity of life extends beyond humans.

Christians attend services to thank God for the harvest

A motion agreed at the Church of England General Synod urged the UK government to do all in its power to ensure that the Earth's resources were used fairly and economically, and to limit the damage caused by pollution. Many Anglican churches are now eco-churches with strict policies on heating and lighting.

The Christian Ecology Link was founded in 1981 as an interdenominational group that informs Christians about environmental issues. Charities like CAFOD, Christian Aid and Tearfund are involved with these issues as well as with global poverty because they are interlinked.

In 1986, Christian leaders met representatives from other world religions at Assisi, the birthplace of **St Francis of Assisi**, to discuss environmental issues. They produced the **Assisi Declarations**, a set of statements on beliefs about the Earth and commitment to environmental conservation.

Many Christians are prepared to accept protest as a way of encouraging change, provided it is non-violent and keeps within the law. Some, however, see minor law-breaking such as trespassing or damaging property as justified in extreme cases. Christians who support this approach might point to the example of Jesus who overturned the traders' tables in the temple in protest at its misuse.

### Key words

**Assisi Declarations**
Statements relating to the environment made by leaders of world religions

**St Francis of Assisi**
Patron saint of animals and a role model for environmental concern

# Questions and activities

## Sample questions and answers

**1** What do Christians mean by stewardship?                    (1 mark)

Being entrusted to look after the world in which they live.

### Commentary

Only 1 mark is available, so a basic answer is sufficient.

**2** Give three ways in which humans might look after the
environment.                                                      (3 marks)

Recycling, not throwing litter, using less electricity.

### Commentary

There are 3 marks for three pieces of information, so three words or phrases are enough.

**3** Explain why many Christians would disagree with the
violent actions of some environmental activists.                 (3 marks)

The teachings of Jesus and Paul do not support violence. When he was being arrested, Jesus said that those who live by the sword die by it. Paul said that Christians should keep the law. Violence harms others, which goes against Christian beliefs.

### Commentary

The command word is 'explain', which means that 3 marks cannot be gained by writing a list. This requires one or two points with development.

**4** 'What's the point in using my car less? One person can't
make a difference to the environment.' Do you agree?
Give reasons for your answer, showing that you have
thought about more than one point of view. Refer to
Christian teachings in your answer.                              (6 marks)

The problems facing our environment are so great that only total commitment to change by governments can save the world from total disaster. The evidence of climate change is there for all to see. Glaciers are disappearing, flooding is more common and hurricanes are more frequent and powerful than ever before. All countries have to make reduction in carbon emissions a national priority. One person cycling rather than driving to work is not going to achieve much, so what's the point?

Having said that, nations are made up of individuals and Christians believe that all individuals have a duty to live responsibly as stewards of the earth. We have all been entrusted with conserving resources by using them sparingly and not greedily, so that the Earth is the beautiful planet that God intended and so that our grandchildren can enjoy it. Even if one person cannot achieve much, it is still our duty to fulfil God's purpose.

I think the quotation shows a self-centred, lazy and defeatist attitude. What's to stop one individual getting together with other individuals and putting pressure on those in power to do something that will be effective? I believe that we live in an amazing world and I think it is up to each of us to keep it that way. The difference one person makes might only be small, but it's still important to make it.

## Commentary

This is an example of an answer where the person writing it feels strongly about an issue. There is no problem with that, providing the writer does not allow his or her views to make the response emotional or incoherent. If you feel strongly about something, you might find it helps to state the other side of the argument first.

## Further questions

**1** Name a Christian organisation that campaigns on environmental issues.      (1 mark)

**2** Explain two environmental problems in the world today.      (4 marks)

**3** Outline the account of creation given in Genesis.      (4 marks)

**4** Explain how religious beliefs and teachings might affect the attitudes of Christians towards the environment.      (5 marks)

## Class activities and homework

### St Francis of Assisi

Research and make notes on the teachings of St Francis that relate to the environment.

Find out what opportunities there are for volunteer work on environmental projects in the UK and elsewhere. Note information about two of these. You may use projects set up by secular or Christian organisations.

## Christians and the environment

Choose a quotation or statement relating to the environment from one of the Christian denominations you are studying. Create for display a poster using that quotation and display relevant images to get across the point being made.

## Your local council

Find out the ways in which your local council is committed to improving the environment. Make a list of what it does. Make another list of anything else you think it should be doing. It may be possible for your teacher to arrange for a local councillor to come in and answer your questions.

Create a 10-point action plan on ways of making your school or college a 'greener' community.

## Useful websites

www.arcworld.org Click on *Projects*, then on *Sacred Gifts: WWF* to gain access to Christian environmental projects.

www.christian-ecology.org.uk

www.shrinkingthefootprint.cofe.anglican.org

www.methodist.org.uk Click on *Open to the World*, then *Environment: Climate Change*.

www.reep.org.uk

www.request.org.uk Click on *Main Site*, then *Basics* and *Environment*.

# World poverty

## The situation

Although only 25% of the world's population live in developed countries, they consume 80% of the world's resources. This suggests that greed and injustice play a part in the issue of global poverty. However, it is a complex problem.

### Natural disasters

Natural disasters such as droughts and hurricanes have always occurred, but climate change is likely to make them more frequent and severe. Their effects are made worse by other factors such as war, corrupt governments, debt and unfair trade.

### Disease

Disease is a huge problem in many developing countries. One of the reasons for this is that pharmaceutical companies in the developed world focus on finding treatments for diseases that are most likely to affect their peoples, such as cancer and heart disease. Therefore, little money is spent on treatments for diseases like leprosy and malaria. Many diseases are caused by polluted water and poor nutrition, but the countries facing these problems are too poor to deal with them by themselves. HIV/AIDS is a serious problem, but for many years the Western pharmaceutical companies would not sell drugs to treat this condition at a price that poor countries could afford.

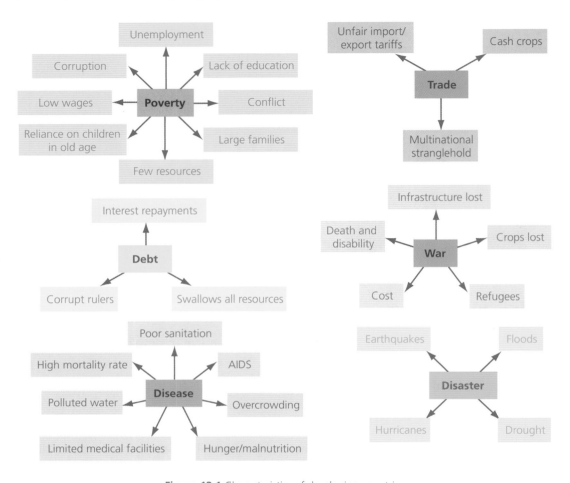

**Figure 12.1** Characteristics of developing countries

## Education

Many children in developing countries receive no education. Their families may need them to work to bring in money or to help on the land, or they may not be able to afford the school fees. Those who do receive education are often in large classes with few resources and little equipment. Girls in particular may be denied an education.

## War

In a war-torn country, money that should be spent on supporting its citizens and building the economy is used to buy weapons and to repair roads and bridges. Those

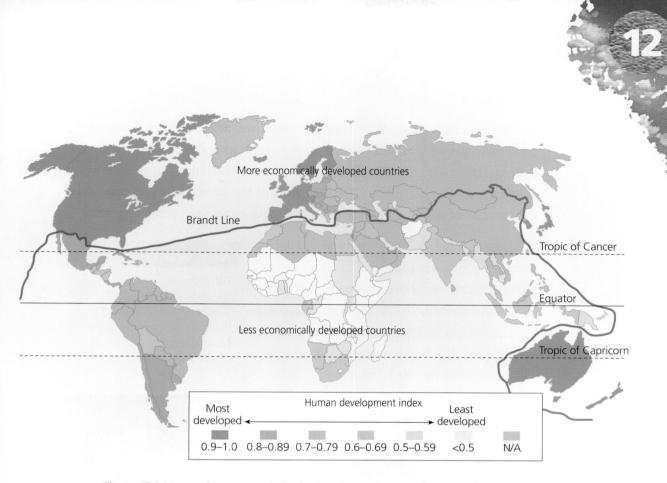

**Figure 12.2** More and less economically developed countries, according to the human development index

who work on the land may be either mercilessly slaughtered or forced into rebel armies, or they may flee to the towns to live on the streets or in shanty towns. In some cases, they escape into neighbouring countries, where they become refugees.

## Debt

Many developing countries are crippled by debt. In the 1970s economic boom, Western governments and banks lent money to poorer countries that was often wasted on fighting wars and providing a luxurious lifestyle for their corrupt rulers. These countries have since experienced difficulties in repaying their debts. There have been major campaigns to pressurise world governments and financial institutions to cancel the debts. In Britain recently, there have been demonstrations and a great deal of pressure put on the government to improve the situation. Some of the debts were cancelled as a result.

## Unfair trade

Wealthy, developed countries hold most of the power when it comes to negotiating trade rules at meetings of the World Trade Organization (WTO). Governments of these countries want to support the best interests of multinational businesses which contribute to their economies. The **G8 summit** has been accused of promoting the interests of powerful Western countries at the expense of poorer countries.

Meanwhile, much of the farming in developing countries is aimed at producing cash crops to pay off national debt rather than providing food for their citizens. Another problem for farmers is that cheap produce is imported from developed countries that want to get rid of their surplus, and local farmers cannot compete with such low prices.

**Key word**

**G8 summit**
An annual meeting of leaders from the world's eight most powerful countries to discuss trade issues and world poverty

Edinburgh Rally 2 July 2005

A Make Poverty History march during the G8 summit in Edinburgh, 2005

## Bad governments

Greed, corruption or incompetence on the part of its government can mean that any income a poor country receives does not benefit those in need. For example, instead of being spent on new hospitals and schools, the money is spent on building a grander palace for the president. Sometimes a nation's revenue is spent on a war against its own people, as in the Darfur region of Sudan. Governments may also avoid tackling problems such as HIV/AIDS.

## Population problems

The world's population has grown enormously over the past 50 years, and there are concerns that there will be insufficient resources for all. In developing countries, families often have large numbers of children for several reasons:

- The lack of state benefits means that people are dependent on their children in old age.
- There is a high infant mortality rate, so parents may wish to have more children in case some of them die during childhood.
- Children are needed to help with farming and looking after animals.
- There is ignorance about or lack of access to contraception.
- There are religious or cultural objections to contraception.

# The response

Some governments are responding to the crisis, although more needs to be done. In the UK, there is a government department for international development that aims to promote sustainable development and eliminate world poverty. A small percentage of the national income is given to projects that focus on reducing poverty. At times of crisis, such as the 2004 Asian tsunami, larger sums are given for immediate relief.

Much of the response to world poverty comes from charities. There are many of these charities in Britain, some of which combine campaigning in the UK with involvement in particular projects in developing countries. Some charities are religious organisations whereas others are secular.

Individuals can also get involved in a variety of ways:

- give money and items that are needed
- give time by working as a volunteer in a charity shop
- raise funds through participating in sponsored events
- become involved in campaigns, e.g. the Make Poverty History protest outside the G8 summit, or letter-writing campaigns to pressurise the government into action on poverty issues
- raise awareness by informing others
- gain skills that are needed in developing countries, and then work in one of these countries
- take time out of regular employment to work on a project in a developing country
- take part in voluntary work while travelling, e.g. during a gap year
- pray for people in need and those working with them

An organisation that has grown considerably in the past decade is the Fairtrade Foundation. Those involved in the **fair-trade** movement aim at getting a fair price for producers in poor countries. Many supermarkets now sell fair-trade produce such as coffee, tea and bananas. The price might be slightly higher than conventional items, but a much greater proportion of the money paid by the final consumer goes directly to the farmer or producer of the goods. Individuals who buy fair-trade products are assisting the campaign for justice for the world's poor.

## Key word

**Fair trade**
A movement that ensures that the disadvantaged growers or producers in the developing world get a fair price for their goods

Fair trade is about better prices, decent working conditions, local sustainability and fair terms of trade for farmers and workers in the developing world

Co-operative group

# Christian attitudes to world poverty

All Christians want to see an end to world poverty. As stated at the start of the previous section, they stress the importance of stewardship and justice. Compassion is also a key principle and Christians believe that they should follow the example of Jesus, whose life and teaching showed his deep concern for the poor.

Some Christians practise tithing, which means they give a tenth of their surplus income to religious and charitable causes. Others do not give a set amount but support particular charities. Many Christians give up what they regard as luxuries during Lent and donate the money they would have spent on them to the poor. Some churches organise weekly Lenten lunches. Those who come are given soup and a bread roll, and the money they would have spent on a meal is given to an organisation such as Christian Aid. One Christian denomination, The Salvation Army, is noted for its work with the poor both in the UK and around the world.

You need to know about the work of one of the following Christian organisations: Christian Aid, CAFOD, Trócaire or Tearfund. The ways in which they work vary, but they are all concerned with:

- long-term aid through projects intended to enable communities in developing countries to become self-sufficient
- short-term or emergency relief
- campaigning to change attitudes in government and big businesses
- producing educational materials for schools and churches
- raising awareness through advertising and websites aimed at both adults and children
- fundraising

Christian Aid was set up to deal with the problem of refugees in Europe at the end of the Second World War, but since then has adapted to meet need on a global scale. It is interdenominational and is increasingly concerned with campaigning and highlighting justice issues as well as providing emergency and long-term aid. Christian Aid is part of the Make Poverty History campaign and the fair-trade movement. It helps whoever is in need, regardless of race, religion and culture. It works through partners, i.e. local groups and organisations in the communities being helped, as these know best what kind of support is needed.

Many Roman Catholics donate to CAFOD. This charity distributes money raised in England and Wales to various projects. It provides both emergency and long-term aid, working (like Christian Aid) through partners in the countries that need support. It is involved in campaigning and raising awareness through education, and is part of the Make Poverty History campaign and the fair-trade movement.

Trócaire was founded by the Roman Catholic Church in Ireland in 1973. It provides long-term and emergency aid, and raises awareness in communities and schools throughout Ireland. It works with partner organisations in developing countries and is involved in a wide range of projects.

Tearfund is a Protestant organisation that works with many different churches throughout the world, providing long-term and emergency aid. It aims to meet the spiritual and physical needs of the poor. It evolved gradually in the 1960s and, like other aid agencies, also works to raise awareness in the UK.

Christian aid agencies and individual Christians are motivated to help others by biblical teaching. In the Old Testament, Jews are commanded to take care of the most vulnerable members of society, and a number of practices were established to help the poor. The New Testament states, 'If anyone has material possessions and sees his brother in need but has no pity on him, how can the love of God be in him?' (1 John 3:17).

This passage reflects the teaching of Jesus that the two greatest commandments are to love God and your neighbour. In his parable of the Good Samaritan, Jesus showed that a person's neighbour is anyone in need, regardless of race, religion, culture, etc. In the parables of the rich fool (Luke 12:16–21), and the rich man and Lazarus (Luke 16:19–31), Jesus told his listeners to respond to those in need and to use their wealth to benefit others.

The rich fool's hoarded wealth was of no use to him when he died suddenly in the night; he would have been better off sharing it and receiving God's reward of eternal life. The rich man who consistently ignored the beggar Lazarus found himself cut off from God after death, and was told that he should have known better. These two parables are clear warnings to Christians that they will be judged, not on whether they have gone to church each week, but on how they have treated those in need. This was made even clearer by Jesus in his parable of the sheep and the goats (Matthew 25:31–46).

# Questions and activities

## Sample questions and answers

**1** Name two countries that are classed as developing countries. (2 marks)

 Tanzania and Bangladesh.

### Commentary

Two names are all that is required. This question is simply testing factual knowledge.

**2** Explain the difference between short-term (emergency) relief and long-term aid. (2 marks)

Short-term relief is aid that is given in response to a particular crisis, such as an earthquake. It is given for a relatively short period of time. Long-term aid refers to projects that are aimed at making individuals and communities self-sufficient and no longer dependent on charity.

### Commentary

As there are only 2 marks, a detailed answer is not necessary. You just need to show your understanding of the difference between the two types of aid.

**3** Explain two reasons for poverty in developing countries. (4 marks)

 One reason for poverty is debt. Many countries borrowed money a few decades ago from institutions in the developed world. When interest rates later soared, they were unable to repay the money. Another reason for poverty is war. Many people become refugees when they try to escape the fighting.

## Commentary

There are two marks for each reason, which means that a reason followed by a simple development is needed. Again, there is no need for a long answer.

## 4 Explain how an individual Christian might help the poor.

(4 marks)

Christians can help the poor in many ways. Those who are unable to give money because they cannot afford it, or those who cannot be actively involved because they are ill or disabled, can pray for the poor and for the people trying to help them. Christians believe that God hears and answers their prayers. They can become involved in the work of an organisation like Christian Aid by organising fundraising activities in their communities and creating greater awareness of the needs of the poor and what Christian Aid does in countries such as Chad. Gap-year students could become volunteers, working on a secular or Christian project in the developing world. Above all, parents can ensure that their children grow up to desire justice for the poor and to see themselves as stewards rather than owners of their wealth, with a duty to use it wisely for the good of all humanity.

## Commentary

This question requires detailed comment on several ways in which the poor might be helped. In view of the word 'Christian' in the question, it is important that there is some religious content in the answer.

## Further questions

**1** Explain why Christians think they should help the poor.　　　　　　(5 marks)

**2** Describe the work of one Christian voluntary agency.　　　　　　(5 marks)

**3** 'Countries are only poor because they have bad governments. They should sort out their problems themselves.' Do you agree? Give reasons for your answer, showing that you have thought about more than one point of view. Refer to Christian teaching in your answer.　　　　　　(6 marks)

## Class activities and homework

### Aid agencies

Find out more about the Christian voluntary agencies you are studying. Create an A4-size poster on each, giving information about the organisation in a way that will be eye-catching and will encourage people to think about becoming involved.

Your teacher will divide the class into groups and give each group an aid project to research. Prepare a short talk for the rest of the class on that project.

Using the websites suggested below, find out more about recent and current campaigns to abolish debt and unfair trade.

### Fair trade

Play one of the fair-trade games produced by Christian Aid or CAFOD. Discuss in groups or as a whole class how you felt as you played and what you have learned.

Research and make bullet point notes on the aims and activities of Traidcraft.

## Useful websites

www.cafod.org.uk

www.christianaid.org.uk

www.fairtrade.org.uk

www.jubileedebtcampaign.org.uk

www.makepovertyhistory.org

www.miniature-earth.com

www.request.org.uk Click on *Main Site*, then *Action*, for information on Christian aid agencies. Click on *Issues*, then *A–Z of Issues* and *Poverty*.

www.sendmyfriend.org

www.tearfund.org

www.traidcraft.co.uk

# Conflict

# Introduction

This short section is an introduction to the next two sections, which deal with crime and punishment, and war and peace. You must study both these topics in relation to the following Christian principles:

- justice
- forgiveness
- reconciliation
- peace

## Justice

Justice is a key Christian principle. It means that each individual has the right to fair, equal and respectful treatment.

With regard to crime and punishment, justice applies to both the victim and the offender. The victim should feel that the hurt or loss he or she has suffered has been taken fully into account. The offender has the right to a fair trial, to being presumed innocent until proved guilty and, if convicted, to a fair punishment. Justice may mean that punishment has to be given, but it should not be seen as a form of revenge.

Justice is important in relation to war and peace. In modern times, the Just War theory applies the idea of justice to conflict situations. However, pacifists argue that war is always unjust.

# Forgiveness

People often misunderstand what is meant by **forgiveness**. They think it is the same as forgetting what has happened. Methodist preacher Gordon Wilson publicly forgave the IRA terrorists whose bomb at the Enniskillen Remembrance Day ceremony killed his daughter, Marie. Gordon never forgot his daughter, but he was able to forgive her killers. Some people think that forgiving a murderer means not handing out punishment, which again seems wrong, especially if the killing was coldly planned beforehand. Some form of punishment may be right and may be needed if justice is to be done. However, forgiveness can affect how the punishment is carried out and how the person being punished feels.

> ### Key word
>
> **Forgiveness**
> Pardoning someone for what they have done and not holding it against them

Forgiveness means a variety of things. For many, it is an ongoing process that may include recurring anger about the hurt that has been caused. It can also mean a refusal to seek revenge or to let hatred fester inside oneself. It means a willingness to move on instead of being locked into a cycle of bitterness.

For Christians, forgiveness is at the heart of their faith. Jesus told his disciples to love their enemies and pray for their persecutors (Matthew 5:44). In his parable of the unmerciful servant (Matthew 18:23-35) he said that God forgives unconditionally and that to be in a position to receive that forgiveness, people must themselves be willing to forgive. As he was nailed to the cross, Jesus asked God to forgive his executioners.

# Reconciliation

Reconciliation means making up with someone. It is not always easy, especially if you are the one who has been hurt, but Jesus' teaching stresses this principle. Christians believe that his death on the cross was the supreme act of reconciliation, tearing down the barrier of sin that separated God and humanity.

Christians believe that any punishment should make reconciliation possible. Some forms of punishment are more likely to achieve this than others. The process of reconciliation leads to the healing of wounds and the possibility of moving on.

This has been seen especially in the work of South Africa's Truth and Reconciliation Commission, where people who committed terrible crimes in the apartheid period met up with their victims. It is also seen in the restorative justice programmes used in some areas of the UK, in which victims of crime have the opportunity to meet those responsible, both to find out why the crime was committed and to make the offender understand the hurt caused.

Christians argue that reconciliation plays an important part in preventing war and healing emotional wounds after a conflict. For example, when Coventry Cathedral was bombed by the German air force in 1940, there was no desire for revenge and no bitterness on the part of the cathedral staff. Two pieces of charred wood that had fallen in the shape of a cross were set up in the ruined building, with the words 'Father, forgive'. It is still there today. At the end of the war, nail crosses were sent as symbols of reconciliation to three German cities that the UK and its allies had bombed.

The Community of the Cross of Nails, an international movement of reconciliation, was started as a result of the bombing of Coventry Cathedral

# Peace

The hope for **peace** is found often in both the Old and New Testaments. The prophet Isaiah longed for an end to conflict and injustice, and the establishment of peace: 'Nation will not take up sword against nation…' (Isaiah 2:4).

Jesus himself said to his disciples, 'Peace I leave with you…' (John 14:27) and 'Blessed are the peacemakers' (Matthew 5:9).

Peace is more than just an absence of fighting; it is a state of wellbeing, of spiritual wholeness. Peace means all people having the right to develop their potential, free from fear of harm.

Christians seek to create a society where people are able to live secure and fulfilled lives. Prison chaplains try to work with inmates, enabling them to come to terms with what they have done, to regret the hurt it caused others and to make a fresh start in which they are at peace with themselves and society.

Pacifists believe that peace means never engaging in conflict, which can be achieved only by finding other ways of dealing with a dispute. Others, however, think that war is sometimes the lesser of two evils and that it can be the only way of establishing long-term peace.

## Questions and activities

### Class activities and homework

#### Forgiveness

Your teacher will divide your class into pairs and assign to each of you one of the people featured on the Forgiveness Project website (www.theforgivenessproject.com). Prepare a short talk for the rest of the class on the experiences of the person or group assigned to you, explaining what the word 'forgiveness' means in that situation.

## Justice and peace

Think about how justice and peace go together. It might help you to read Isaiah 2:2–4; 9:6–7; 11:2–9. Create a poster to express your ideas.

Make notes on the Community of the Cross of Nails (CCN).

## Useful websites

www.coventrycathedral.org.uk Click on *Our Reconciliation Ministry*.

www.crossofnails.org

www.theforgivenessproject.com

# War and peace

## Causes of war

Wars are usually fought to gain wealth or power, or for better trading opportunities. Sometimes wars are fought out of revenge, if a previous conflict ended badly for one side or the peace terms were humiliating. Many wars in the past were fought because of imperialism — the desire to conquer and rule as much of the world as possible.

Some modern conflicts have been ideological, to assert a particular way of life or set of beliefs. They may have political, nationalist or religious goals. Wars may be fought as a response to acts of aggression or to protect human rights.

## Types of weapons and warfare

There are many different types of weapons and warfare. Most wars rely on conventional weapons, e.g. guided missiles, cluster

In some wars, children are made to fight and kill

bombs and land mines. Huge amounts of money are spent on improving weapons and developing new types and Britain is a major arms exporter.

Chemical and biological weapons are banned in internationally agreed treaties, but both have been developed by many nations and used by a few. For example, in the Vietnam War the USA used napalm, which causes terrible burns.

## Nuclear warfare and proliferation

In August 1945, the USA dropped atomic bombs on Hiroshima and Nagasaki in Japan, leading to the end of the Second World War in Asia. Hundreds of thousands of civilians died, radioactive gases are still present in the atmosphere and deformed babies are still being born. The USA justified this action by saying that it ended the Second World War more quickly. Today's nuclear weapons are much more powerful than those used in 1945 and their use would be devastating.

Nuclear proliferation, i.e. the increasing number of countries developing nuclear weapons, is a major concern, and there are fears that irresponsible governments or terrorists might obtain them.

The destruction of the Twin Towers on 9/11

# Terrorism

Terrorism refers to actions of extreme violence in pursuit of political aims. Sometimes terrorists target those they blame for injustice and oppression, such as the government of a particular country, but they usually extend their action to include innocent people. This is to achieve maximum publicity and terrify the public. Those motivated by religion believe they are doing God's will. Suicide bombers believe they will be transported to paradise immediately, without any wait for the Day of Judgement. Present-day terrorism is most commonly associated with Al Qaeda-linked groups, such as those responsible for 9/11 (New York) and 7/7 (London).

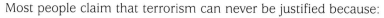

Most people claim that terrorism can never be justified because:

- The violence is indiscriminate and ruthless.
- It is a weapon of fear and coercion.
- It exploits the innocent to promote its purpose.

However, some people believe that on rare occasions there is no alternative to terrorism. For oppressed people who have tried every other means of putting right the injustice they suffer, such violence is seen as the only way of making the world take notice.

# The Just War theory

**Key word**

**Just War theory**
Set of conditions to be met if war is to be justified

Although war is never a good thing, there may be occasions when it is justified. A simple form of the **Just War theory** was in existence before the birth of Christ, but the Christian Church developed it over the centuries. It continues to be used as a standard by many people today, including politicians and journalists. There are eight criteria and each of them must be satisfied if the war is to be 'just'. In practice this is usually impossible so only the most important criteria need to be met.

For a war to be just, it must be fought:

- by a proper authority — a just war is one that has been declared by the ruler of the country concerned
- in a just cause — this is restricted to defence
- with right intent — the aims must be just and, once these have been achieved, the war must stop
- with reasonable chance of success — it is wrong for thousands to be killed in a war that has little chance of being won
- to ensure a better future than could be expected without a war — there is no point to a war if victory will not improve things
- as a last resort — everything possible must be tried to avoid going to war, such as talks, pressure from the United Nations and sanctions
- by just means — there must be no deliberate killing of civilians and the innocent
- with proportionate force — excessive use of force is not permissible

# Pacifism

Many people, including atheists and agnostics as well as religious believers, are **pacifist**. They believe that violence against other human beings is wrong. They are totally opposed to war, believing that it can never be justified.

**Key word**

**Pacifist**
Someone who is
opposed to violence

Some of the arguments for and against pacifism are set out in Table 14.1.

**Table 14.1** Arguments for and against pacifism

| Arguments for pacifism | Arguments against pacifism |
| --- | --- |
| **Beliefs about human life**<br>■ everyone has the right to life<br>■ life is sacred<br>■ lives should be treated with respect<br>■ all are part of the human family | **The right to life is not absolute**<br>■ an aggressor has forfeited that right by the act of aggression<br>■ some lives may be sacrificed to protect others |
| **War causes immense suffering**<br>■ modern methods of fighting harm the innocent<br>■ the suffering caused is out of all proportion to the evil being fought<br>■ the suffering may affect future generations | **War limits suffering**<br>■ it can defend and protect the innocent<br>■ the 'just' war conditions ensure proportional violence<br>■ refusal to fight may make aggressors think they can do whatever they want, and this may result in more suffering |
| **War is a waste of resources**<br>■ the money spent on weapons would solve social problems and meet some global needs<br>■ money should be spent on saving lives, not destroying them<br>■ it causes irreparable damage to the environment<br>■ it uses up precious minerals and other resources | **War can be a wise use of resources**<br>■ wars that are fought to end injustice may save resources in the long run because greedy oppressors waste resources |
| **War brings out the worst in people**<br>■ e.g. greed and prejudice | **War brings out the best in people**<br>■ e.g. courage and compassion |

# Christian attitudes to war and peace

In the early centuries of the Church, it was pacifist. Today one denomination, the Religious Society of Friends (Quakers), still is. Many Christians from other denominations are also pacifist and they may belong to a Christian pacifist group such as Pax Christi. Christian pacifists believe that everyone is a child of God and should never be harmed by a fellow human being. All humans are in the image of God and their bodies are 'temples of the Holy Spirit'. Life is a precious gift from God. Christians quote texts from the New Testament, especially the Gospels, where Jesus encouraged forgiveness and reconciliation as the way to solve problems. Some of these were outlined in Section 13.

Christians who are not pacifist believe that Jesus' teaching should not be taken literally. They point to Paul's letter to the Romans in which he stated that the civil authorities should be obeyed as their power was God-given. The Catechism of the Catholic Church states that while avoidance of conflict is the ideal, sometimes war is necessary. The Catechism supports the Just War theory, as do most other Christians who are not pacifist.

Dietrich Bonhoeffer was a German theologian who lived at the time of Hitler's rise to power. He was a devout Christian and was originally a pacifist. He formed the 'Confessing Church', which opposed the government and helped to get Jews out of Germany. He was imprisoned and after his release he joined a secret resistance movement. He came to the conclusion that only violent action would defeat Hitler. He was arrested again and eventually executed in 1945, just a

Dietrich Bonhoeffer

## Key word

**Martyr**
Someone who dies for his or her faith

few weeks before Germany surrendered. In Canterbury Cathedral, Bonhoeffer is commemorated in a chapel dedicated to twentieth-century **martyrs**. In Westminster Abbey his statue can be seen on the west front, along with other modern martyrs.

**Campaign for Nuclear Disarmament (CND)**
An organisation that supports unilateral disarmament

All Christians, whether pacifist or not, are concerned about the arms race and the threat posed by nuclear weapons. Many belong to the **Campaign for Nuclear Disarmament**. Pope John XXIII spoke out against nuclear weapons in 1963 and some years later an Anglican report called *The Church and the Bomb* encouraged the British government to get rid of its nuclear weapons, whatever the attitude of other countries. Many Christians denounce the billions of pounds spent on weapons of destruction that could instead be saving lives.

# Questions and activities

## Sample questions and answers

### 1 Where was the first nuclear bomb dropped? (1 mark)

Hiroshima.

### Commentary

Only the place name is needed.

### 2 Explain what Christians mean by a 'just' war. (5 marks)

For a war to be a just war, it must fulfil a number of conditions. One of these is that it must be fought in a just cause, i.e. it must be a war of defence. Britain went to war against Germany in the Second World War because Hitler invaded Poland. Poland was an ally, so Britain went to its defence. Another condition is that the war must be a last resort. Before war broke out in 1939, Britain had tried to sort things out peacefully. Neville Chamberlain returned from talks with Hitler waving a signed agreement. He believed he had secured 'Peace for our time'. When Hitler broke that treaty, it was felt that nothing other than war would stop him.

Two other conditions are concerned with the way the war is fought: civilians should not be harmed and the amount of force used must not be excessive. Many people today think that these conditions were broken by Britain and the USA in the Second World War when the German city of Dresden was bombed and when nuclear bombs were dropped on Hiroshima and Nagasaki. Thousands of civilians were killed and extreme violence was used.

## Commentary

The command word 'explain' means that your answer should be more than just a list of conditions. Here, four conditions have been given, with examples to explain what the terms mean. In the last two sentences, an opinion (held by many people) is given, but it does not turn this into an evaluation question. The opinion is used to explain what 'just' and 'proportionate force' mean.

**3** 'Christians who go to war are hypocrites.' Do you agree? Give reasons for your answer, showing that you have thought about more than one point of view. Refer to Christian teachings in your answer. (5 marks)

I can see why some people think this. Christians of all denominations believe that peace is important and killing is never a good thing. The sixth Commandment (for Roman Catholics, the fifth) states 'Do not kill.' Many Christians are pacifist and believe that by refusing to go to war they are following the teaching of Jesus, who said 'Turn the other cheek' and 'Love your neighbour as yourself'. He told his disciples that those who live by the sword die by it, which means that violence creates more violence.

However, some Christians point out that 'do not kill' refers to unjustified killing such as murder, and believe that war entails killing in a just cause. Jesus said, 'Blessed are the peacemakers' and it could be argued that sometimes peace can be effectively made only through some use of force. For many Christians, war is never a good thing but it may be the lesser of two evils. They argue that religious believers who go to war are hypocrites only if they do so for selfish reasons and if they do it in a spirit of revenge. Personally, I think that it is not hypocritical to be involved in a war providing you keep the principles of your faith in mind and fight only in order to make something good come out of evil.

## Commentary

Two sides are discussed in some detail here. Note the instruction to include Christian teaching. Without this, the answer would reach no more than Level 3.

## Further questions

**1** What is terrorism?                                                    (2 marks)

**2** Explain how a Christian might apply the idea of sanctity of life to the
issue of war and peace.                                                     (3 marks)

**3** Explain why some Christians are pacifist.                             (5 marks)

## Class activities and homework

### Dietrich Bonhoeffer

In pairs or small groups, find out more about Dietrich Bonhoeffer. Imagine you are
able to conduct an interview with him. With one group acting as Dietrich
Bonhoeffer, think of some questions you might ask him. Your teacher will allocate
roles so that each group has a different perspective. Possible roles are a member
of the Nazi party, a member of Hitler's family, an ordinary German who sees Hitler
as the 'saviour' of his people, one of Bonhoeffer's prison guards, Bonhoeffer's
fiancée, a Christian pacifist, a Jew who escaped from Nazi persecution.

### Just War theory

Find or write a summary of the causes, progress and ending of a particular war.
Create a table with two columns, the first headed 'Just War' and the other 'Example'.
In the first column, list the conditions given on page 125. In the second column,
next to each of the conditions give an example from the war you have summarised
showing how the countries involved fulfilled or broke that condition.

Find out about the work of the Campaign against Arms Trade at
www.caat.org.uk. Research the cost of weapons and which countries are
the major arms suppliers.

### War and peace film

Watch an entire film or clips from a film that raise issues of war and peace or civil
disobedience, such as *Gandhi* or *Saving Private Ryan*.

## Christian pacifism

In pairs, research a Christian pacifist organisation and create a flyer informing the public about its beliefs and work.

Research in detail the life of a famous Christian who worked for peace by non-violent means. Write a side of A4 to show how he or she did this. Try not to give just a biography of the person, choose examples to show how he or she used non-violence to achieve peace.

Write a concluding paragraph to state whether or not you think he or she was successful.

## Useful websites

www.anglicanpeacemaker.org.uk

www.baptist-peace.org.uk

www.caat.org.uk

www.chipspeace.org

www.corrymeela.org

www.coventrycathedral.org.uk

www.cptuk.org.uk

http://news.bbc.co.uk

www.paxchristi.org.uk

www.quaker.org.uk

www.yap.org

# Crime and punishment

## Crime

A **crime** is an offence committed in breach of the law of the land. Crimes may be committed against:

- a person, e.g. grievous bodily harm (GBH)
- property, e.g. vandalism
- the state, e.g. treason

**Key word**

**Crime**
An offence committed against the law of the land

Crime is a problem in Britain. The rate of recorded crime is dropping, but violent crime and robbery are on the increase. Men are far more likely to commit crime than women, and most criminals are in their late teens.

## Why do people commit crime?

The reasons for committing crime are usually:

- social — the community someone mixes with or is influenced by
- environmental — someone's background and circumstances
- psychological — someone's personality and emotional state

There is debate about whether crime is a result of 'nature' or 'nurture', i.e. whether people are born with a tendency to be good or bad, or whether it depends on how they are brought up. Many people would argue that free will plays a part.

Some of the causes of crime are:

- alcohol and drug addiction
- poverty
- boredom
- peer pressure
- bad parental example
- emotional reactions such as anger or jealousy
- rebellion
- greed

# Aims of punishment

Those who are found guilty of offences are usually punished. Before deciding on a particular punishment magistrates and judges think about why they are giving it and what they hope to achieve by it. What purpose does it serve? There are four main aims of punishment:

- Deterrence — when a punishment is given to discourage the offender from committing crime again, and to discourage others who might be tempted to commit the same crime.
- Protection — law-abiding people need to feel safe. Victims of crime and frail or elderly people often feel insecure. Sometimes offenders with a mental illness need to be kept in secure accommodation in order to prevent them from committing an offence.
- Reformation — changing offenders' attitudes towards themselves and others so they no longer want to offend, but to contribute to society in a positive way.
- Retribution — often summed up in the biblical phrase 'an eye for an eye'. Retribution means giving a punishment proportionate to the crime. However, it can easily slide into revenge.

# Forms of punishment

There are many different punishments available, depending on:

- the severity of the crime
- the nature and circumstances of the offender

## Imprisonment

The prison rate is higher in Britain than anywhere else in Europe and overcrowding is a serious problem. Conditions in many prisons are terrible, and some prisoners have to 'slop out' (empty chamber pots). Prisoners may be locked up for almost the whole time, with limited exercise and few opportunities for education or work. Bullying and assault are major issues, and suicide, attempted suicide and self-harm are common. The reoffending rate is high.

Young people who need to be kept in custody may be put in:

- young offender institutions (YOIs)
- secure training centres
- secure children's homes

## Community service

Community service is one of the many supervision orders that benefit the community. Offenders have to do unpaid work in their own time for a set number of hours.

## Fines

These are paid to the court and are given for motoring and some other offences.

Young offenders doing community work by painting a wall covered with graffiti

Janine Wiedel Photolibrary/Alamy

# The death penalty (capital punishment)

In 1965, **capital punishment** for murder was suspended for 5 years. In 1970, it was abolished. As a member state of the European Union, Britain is committed to a policy of not having a death penalty. Nevertheless, if it were put to a public referendum, the majority of British citizens would almost certainly support the death penalty for certain types of murder.

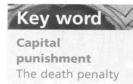

**Key word**

Capital
punishment
The death penalty

Worldwide, countries are gradually abolishing the death penalty, though many do still use it, for example China and the USA.

## Arguments for and against the death penalty

Secular arguments for and against the death penalty are given below. Christians use some of them alongside more explicitly religious points.

Arguments in favour of restoring the death penalty:

- Society would be protected. 'Life imprisonment' is not usually lifelong.
- It would act as a deterrent.
- A victim's family can be satisfied that justice has been done and this can help them to move on.
- It shows society's total abhorrence of murder and stops Britain from becoming uncivilised.
- It is a form of reparation. In a sense, the death of a murderer is compensation to society for the loss of one of its members.
- Improved forensic science makes it unlikely that innocent people will be executed.
- The death penalty is kinder to a murderer than a lifetime of prison and guilt.

Arguments against restoring the death penalty:

- Release from prison is always on licence, which means that murderers may be recalled at any time and their whereabouts are always known.
- The example of the USA shows that the death penalty does not deter murderers.
- If terrorists were put to death they would be seen as martyrs.
- It can too easily become a form of revenge.

- There is a possibility of innocent people being executed. Forensic science is only as good as the scientists using it.
- It prevents repentance and reform. Some 'lifers' have made an important contribution to society.
- It reduces society to the level of the murderer and shows a lack of respect for life.
- It harms others, encouraging feelings of revenge in the victim's family and punishing the family of the murderer.
- It is costly because the legal processes, such as appeals, are expensive.

# Christian attitudes to crime and punishment

## The law

All Christians believe that, to uphold a stable society, the law of the land should be obeyed unless it is morally wrong. Jesus himself said: 'Give to Caesar what is Caesar's and to God what is God's' (Mark 12:17). He clearly thought that there were duties to the state.

When there is a conflict between duties to the state and to God, Christians have taken Jesus' words as meaning that God should come first. There are examples throughout history of Christians taking a stand against unjust governments, for example Martin Luther King Jr in the USA, Dietrich Bonhoeffer in Nazi Germany, Oscar Romero in El Salvador and Desmond Tutu during apartheid in South Africa.

## Punishment of offenders

Christians accept that punishment may be necessary. Crime hurts its victims, and offenders need to know that. They also need to learn respect for the law as guaranteeing the rights of others.

Punishment should always go hand in hand with forgiveness, which is central to Christianity. In the Lord's Prayer, Christians ask God to forgive their sins as they forgive those who sin against them. Jesus told Peter to be prepared to forgive unconditionally and without limit, illustrating this in his parable of the unforgiving servant (Matthew 18:21–35). Christians believe that an unwillingness to forgive damages offenders who are sorry for what they have done and also those who cannot forgive. Bitterness, hatred and the desire for revenge can easily consume a person. Those who are willing to forgive are more able to move on.

For Christians, the most important aim of punishment is reform. People must work with offenders to enable them to change. Christians are conscious that crime is often the result of material or emotional deprivation, and the offender needs help as much as punishment. The process of reform may include the use of restorative justice.

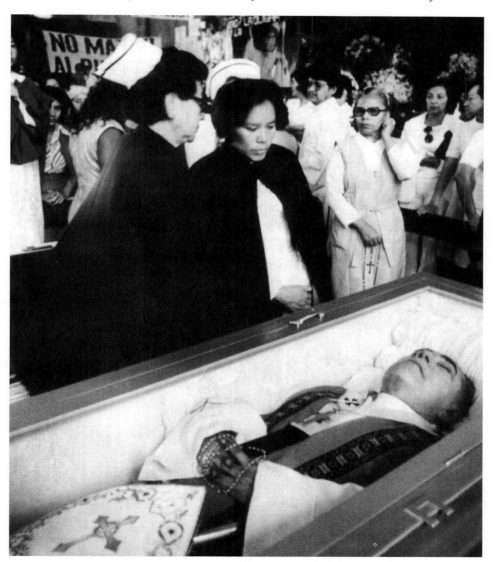

Oscar Romero was shot dead after he called for his country's soldiers to stop carrying out the government's repression

The aim of punishment Christians are least happy about, therefore, is retribution. Some support it as enabling justice to be done and as giving criminals what they deserve. However, retribution can easily degenerate into a desire for retaliation and revenge. This is totally against the spirit of the New Testament. Paul told his fellow Christians never to seek vengeance.

Christians recognise the need to protect society from some individuals. These individuals may also need protection from their own worst instincts through restrictions placed on their freedom.

Attitudes to punishment as a deterrent vary. It seems sensible to have a punishment that will deter potential offenders but treating someone harshly to deter others seems like unjust exploitation. People are then 'frightened' into being law-abiding, and fear is not the most effective method of achieving something.

Christians believe in giving offenders a second chance and offering them friendship. Some write to or visit people in prison, or offer support and friendship to prisoners' families. Christian employers may be willing to give a job to someone who has been in prison. All prisons have chaplains. There are discussion groups, Bible study and regular services.

The Anglican Church supports alternatives to prison as a more effective method of rehabilitation and re-education. It stresses the importance of tackling the sources of crime, especially poverty.

## Capital punishment

Some Christians support capital punishment, following the Old Testament teaching of an eye for an eye and a life for a life. They believe that only the death penalty shows that the law is to be obeyed and respected. The Catechism of the Catholic Church accepts the death penalty for what it terms 'grave offences', but prefers 'bloodless' solutions. Many modern Roman Catholic leaders are totally against the death penalty.

Anglicans and Quakers strongly oppose the death penalty because they believe it serves no useful purpose and is inhumane. There is no possibility of reform or reparation. There is a story about Jesus being asked to pass judgement on a woman caught in the act of adultery, the penalty for which was to be stoned to death. Jesus said that anyone who had committed no sin should throw the first stone. The woman's accusers left and Jesus told the woman that he did not condemn her, but she should not repeat her sin.

# Questions and activities

## Sample questions and answers

**1** Name two types of punishment that might be given by British courts. (2 marks)

 Imprisonment and probation.

### Commentary
Two words are sufficient.

**2** Explain two reasons why people commit crime. (4 marks)

Some people commit crime as a form of protest, for example trespassing on Ministry of Defence land in order to get their anti-war slogans televised. A drug addict may steal something and sell it in order to pay for the drugs he craves.

### Commentary
Two developed reasons are required here. The easiest way of developing a point is by giving an example.

**3** Explain why many Christians are concerned about the state of British prisons. (4 marks)

 Christians believe in the sanctity of life. All human beings should be treated with respect, but conditions in many prisons seem inhumane. In some prisons, 'slopping out' still occurs, which means that inmates have to use buckets in their cells as toilets. People may be locked up for 23 out of 24 hours because there are insufficient prison warders. This prevents the social contact that humans need if they are to function properly and makes

 prisoners feel frustrated. Imprisonment is meant to punish by removing a person's freedom; it is not meant to take away his or her dignity as a human being.

## Commentary

It would be easy to give a secular answer to this question, but that would not be awarded full marks because of the word 'Christians' in the question. There needs to be some religious content in the answer. This can be found in the first few sentences of the answer. The principle of respect for human life is then applied to the issue of prison conditions.

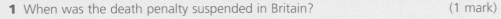

## Further questions

**1** When was the death penalty suspended in Britain?     (1 mark)

**2** Name two countries that still carry out the death penalty.     (2 marks)

**3** Name two crimes that are frequently committed in Britain.     (2 marks)

**4** Explain how Christian beliefs and teachings might influence the attitude of religious believers towards those who commit crimes.     (5 marks)

**5** 'Criminals should not be punished. Their upbringing is responsible for what they do.' Do you agree? Give reasons for your answer, showing that you have thought about more than one point of view. Refer to Christian arguments in your answer.     (6 marks)

## Class activities and homework

### Capital punishment

Prepare for and hold a debate on the motion: 'This class believes that the death penalty is the most appropriate punishment for murderers.' Your teacher will divide the class into four groups, telling you whether you are to support or oppose the motion. One student from each group should present the arguments in the debate. Another student will act as chairperson. The rest of the class should be ready to make points arising out of the debate when invited to do so.

 Make bullet-point notes on the most important issues raised in the debate.

## Organisations that work with prisoners

Your teacher will divide the class into small groups and will allocate to each group an organisation that gives support and help to prisoners. Prepare and give a short presentation to the rest of the class using any medium you wish, such as 'chalk and talk', a PowerPoint presentation or handouts. Use textbooks and leaflets provided by your teacher or carry out your research using the websites suggested below.

Research and make notes on the life and work of Elizabeth Fry, who was involved in the reform of Newgate Prison. What Christian principles motivated her work?

Research different types of sentences that are given in UK courts and suggest crimes for which they would be appropriate punishments

## Useful websites

www.crimeinfo.org.uk

www.howardleague.org

www.internationaljusticeproject.org

www.nacro.org.uk

http://re-xs.ucsm.ac.uk Click on *Ethical & Moral Issues*, then *Crime & Punishment*.

www.storybookdads.co.uk

www.theforgivenessproject.com

# Exam technique

When answering questions, always note:

- the command word
- the number of marks available

## Command words

These tell you the kind of answer that is needed:

- 'Describe' means that you need to give information.
- 'Give' usually requires you to give basic pieces of information or reasons for something.
- 'Explain' requires some comment on facts or beliefs, e.g. 'Explain how religious believers might help the poor.' Do not just give a list, but discuss the points you make. Use examples to help you do this.
- 'What do you think? Explain your opinion.' This requires you to give and justify your opinion on a religious issue.
- 'Do you agree? Give reasons for your answer, showing that you have thought about more than one point of view. Refer to Christian teaching in your answer.' This requires you to argue a case for two different (though not necessarily opposing) points of view and explain why you agree with one of them. If you're not sure where you stand on an issue, don't be afraid to say so, but explain why you either disagree with both arguments or find it hard to decide. To move beyond Level 4 (4 marks out of 6) you have to give two points of view, and to move beyond Level 3 (3 marks out of 6) you have to include Christian argument. You don't have to be a Christian yourself or to agree with the viewpoint, but you need to show that you can see how religious beliefs might affect someone's views on the issue.

## Marks available

These are given at the end of each part of a question and give you some idea about the type of answer required, and how much to write:

- 'What do you think? Explain...' questions are always marked out of 3. You do not need to give more than one viewpoint, and you do not have to write at great length.

- 'Do you agree? Give…' questions are always marked out of 6 and you need to write two (or more) paragraphs and a conclusion or at least two paragraphs in which it is clear what your view is.
- 'Give' questions will be out of 3 marks at the most, and will be asking for one, two or three pieces of information, depending on the number of marks. Don't write at length.
- Questions with 1 mark require a word, phrase or short sentence.
- Where 'describe', 'how', 'why' or 'explain' are used, look at the number of marks available. The more marks, the more you need to write, and the more likely it is that more than a list is required.

## Timing

This is crucial. If you do not have time to answer one or more of the questions, you may end up at least one grade lower. If, for example, you do not have time for the structured essay in Part B, you will lose 24 marks and, even if all your other answers are outstanding, you cannot be awarded more than 48 marks for them out of a total of 72.

- Keep an eye on the clock.
- Where one-word answers are required, write one word.
- If you are unable to answer a question, don't hang about. Go on to the next and come back to it later.
- If you make a mistake, just cross it through and write another answer. Don't neatly cross out each word or line. If you've written a lot, a quick diagonal line through is enough.
- Remember to answer only one of the two essay questions in Part B. You have a choice of which one to answer.

## Quality of written communication (QWC)

This concerns your ability to get across your meaning clearly. The following elements contribute to this: spelling, punctuation, grammar, structure, style and legibility of handwriting. There is no separate mark for QWC. Instead, it is one of the factors taken into account when 6-mark evaluation responses are marked.

# Glossary

## A

**Abortion** The deliberate termination of a pregnancy

**Absolute morality** A type of morality that has fixed and unchanging rules

**Active euthanasia** Deliberately ending the life of someone who is seriously ill

**Adultery** A sexual relationship between two people, at least one of whom is married to someone else

**Advance decisions** These tell medical staff how patients wish to be treated at the end of their lives, should they be unable to communicate their wishes

**African National Congress (ANC)** A political party that was formed to increase the rights of black people in South Africa

**Annulment** The declaration that a valid marriage never existed

**Anti-semitism** Hatred of Jews that expresses itself in discrimination

**Apartheid** The policy of racial segregation and discrimination enforced by the white minority governments of South Africa

**Artificial insemination by husband (AIH)** A form of fertility treatment using the husband's sperm

**Artificial insemination by donor/donor insemination (AID/DI)** A form of fertility treatment using donor sperm

**Assisi Declarations** Statements relating to the environment made by leaders of world religions

**Autonomy** The right to make decisions for yourself

## B

**Black Power** A political movement among African Americans in the USA, which emphasised racial pride and promoted black interests

**British National Party (BNP)** A far-right political party in the UK

## C

**Campaign for Nuclear Disarmament (CND)** An organisation that supports unilateral disarmament

**Capital punishment** The death penalty

**Casual sex** Sex without commitment

**Catechism of the Catholic Church** A book containing the official teaching of the Roman Catholic Church on all matters of faith and practice

**Celibacy** Not having a sexual relationship within or outside marriage, often as a result of a religious promise

**Chastity** Having moral standards and restraint with regard to sexual relations

**Christian denominations** The different Christian traditions, e.g. Anglican, Roman Catholic

**Civil partnership ceremonies** Non-religious ceremonies that allow gay couples to legally register their partnerships

**Civil rights movement** A movement that sought to gain justice for black people in the USA by non-violent means

**Cloning** Creating a genetically identical organism

**Cohabitation** A couple living together and enjoying a sexual relationship without being married

**Commercialisation** Exploiting for the purpose of making a profit

**Contraception** A range of methods that may be used to prevent pregnancy

**Crime** An offence committed against the law of the land

# D

**Designer babies** Babies whose genetic structure has been chosen for certain characteristics

**Discrimination** Putting prejudice into action

# E

**Ensoulment** The point at which the foetus receives its soul from God, and therefore becomes a person

**Eucharist** One of the Christian sacraments, a service at which Christians eat bread and drink wine in remembrance of Jesus' death

**Euthanasia** The deliberate termination of a life in order to end someone's suffering

**Extra-marital sex** A sexual relationship between two people who are not married to each other. They may be single or married to someone else.

# F

**Fair trade** A movement that ensures that disadvantaged growers or producers in the developing world get a fair price for their goods

**Fertility treatment** Given to enable women to conceive

**Foetal rights** The rights of the unborn child

**Forgiveness** Pardoning someone for what they have done and not holding it against them

**Fundamentalist Christian** Someone who believes that the Bible was inspired directly by God and contains no errors. Its teachings are always relevant.

# G

**G8 summit** An annual meeting of leaders from the world's eight most powerful countries to discuss trade issues and world poverty

**Gateway drug** A soft drug that may lead someone on to use hard drugs

**Genetic engineering** Manipulating a person's genetic structure

# H

**Hard drugs** Class A drugs. These cause the most damage and are often addictive.

**Homosexuality** Being attracted to people of the same sex

**Hospice** A place that provides care for terminally ill patients

**Human Fertilisation and Embryology Authority (HFEA)** The committee that regulates all research, etc, relating to the embryo

**Hybrid embryo** Embryo created by putting human genetic material into an empty cow's egg

# I

**Institutional racism** Racial prejudice and discrimination that are said to be at the heart of some organisations

**In vitro fertilisation (IVF)** A form of fertility treatment in which the eggs are fertilised outside the womb

**Islamophobia** Irrational fear of Muslims that leads to discrimination

# J

**Justice** Treating everyone fairly and equally

**Just War theory** Set of conditions to be met if war is to be justified

# K

**Ku Klux Klan (KKK)** A white racist group in the USA

**Kyoto Treaty** An international agreement to cut back on carbon emissions and deal with environmental problems.

# L

**Liberal Christian** Someone who believes that God guided the writers of the Bible, but that there are mistakes and some of its teachings are out of date

# M

**Macmillan nurse** A nurse who is specially trained in palliative care for cancer patients

**Martyr** Someone who dies for his or her faith

**Maternal rights** The rights of the mother

# N

**Non-voluntary euthanasia** Ending the life of a sick person who is incapable of requesting death

**Nuptial Mass** A service of Holy Communion held as part of the marriage ceremony

# P

**Pacifist** Someone who is opposed to violence

**Palliative care** Specialised care that relieves pain and distress

**Passive euthanasia** Letting a person die without medical intervention

**Passive smoking** This is when someone who does not smoke inhales smoke exhaled by someone who does

**Peace** Being able to live without fear of harm and to fulfil your potential

**Permanent vegetative state (PVS)** An irreversible condition caused by the destruction of the neo-cortical area of the brain

**Pre-implantation genetic diagnosis (PGD)** Screening embryos created in IVF treatment to select those that would be the closest match to a sick child

**Prejudice** An irrational opinion about an individual or group

**Pre-marital sex** Sexual intercourse prior to marriage

**Pro-choice** Supporting the right of women to decide for themselves whether or not to have an abortion

**Procreative sex** Sex which has the possibility of conception

**Pro-life** The anti-abortion view that the foetus has absolute right to life

# Q

**Quality of life** Whether or not a person will have a life that is worthwhile and of value

# R

**Reconciliation** One of the Christian sacraments. It involves confessing your sins to a priest and the priest declaring God's forgiveness.

**Relative morality** A type of morality which takes the situation and circumstances into account

**Reproductive cloning** Also known as human cloning, this would be the creation of an identical copy of a human

**Respect for life** Recognising that every living being has value

**Respite care** A short period of rest for carers

**Responsibility** The duties that humans have because of the power they exercise

# S

**Sacrament** An outward action or ceremony that gives a spiritual blessing

**Sacramental covenant** A sacred contract involving promises. It is a binding agreement in which God acts as witness.

**Saint Francis of Assisi** Patron saint of animals and a role model for environmental concern

**Sanctions** Refusing to trade with a country and to supply what it needs

**Sanctity of life** The idea that life is holy and precious

**Saviour siblings** Babies conceived using PGD and IVF, whose cord blood is used to treat seriously ill siblings

**Scapegoating** Blaming an innocent individual or group for something that is wrong

**Secular** Not religious

**Soft drugs** Class B drugs. These are less harmful and less addictive than hard drugs, but are illegal and can cause serious problems.

**Somatic-cell therapy** Correcting a faulty gene through replacing it with a working copy

**Stereotyping** Creating an oversimplified image of an individual or group, usually by assuming that all members of the group are the same

**Stewardship** The idea that humans do not own the world but should look after it responsibly on behalf of God

**Suffragette movement** A reform movement in the early twentieth century that aimed to secure the right for women to vote

**Surrogacy** A woman carrying and giving birth to a child on behalf of another couple

# T

**Teetotal** Not drinking alcohol

**Therapeutic cloning** Also known as stem-cell cloning. This would use stem cells from an embryo to create replacement tissue or organs.

**Trimester** A period of 3 months. Pregnancy is divided into three trimesters.

**Truth and Reconciliation Commission** A body that investigated the crimes committed by both black and white people in South Africa during the apartheid era, in the hope of getting people to face up to what they had done and to seek and receive forgiveness from their victims

# U

**Unitive sex** The idea that sexual intercourse makes a couple one

# V

**Viability** The point in development at which a baby could be born with some chance of independent survival

**Voluntary euthanasia** Ending a person's life at his or her request

# Useful websites

You may find these websites useful throughout your course. Websites that relate to particular topics have been listed at the end of the appropriate sections.

For these sites, use the search engine to direct you to the information that you need:

http://news.bbc.co.uk

www.bbc.co.uk

www.channel4.com

A revision site:

www.bbc.co.uk/schools/gcsebitesize/rs

This site covers world religions, ethical issues and also directs you to other websites:

http://re-xs.ucsm.ac.uk

This site gives information on Christian beliefs, practices and responses to issues. It also gives information on famous Christians:

www.request.org.uk

# Index

Page numbers in **bold** type indicate the main definition of each key word and glossary term.

# C

# D

Darfur, Sudan  *109*
death penalty (capital punishment)  **135**, *136*, *138–39*, **144**
debt  *105, 107, 108*
de Klerk, F. W.  *91*
designer babies  *41*, **42**, *43, 44*, **145**
deterrence  *133, 135, 138*
DI *see* donor insemination
Didache  *15*
Dignity in Dying  *23*
'The Dignity of a Person' (Vatican)  *37, 49*
disability
    abortion  *10, 11, 12, 14, 15, 16*
    discrimination  *87*
    euthanasia  *22*
Disability Discrimination Act (*1995*)  *87*
discrimination  *82–94*
    causes  *83*
    Christian attitudes  *87–89*
    definition  **82**, **145**
    disability discrimination  *87*
    discrimination and the law  *83*
    gender discrimination  *85–86, 88–89*
    Martin Luther King Jr  *89–90*
    Nelson Mandela  *90–91*
    questions and activities  *92–94*
    racial and colour discrimination  *83–84, 88–91*
    religious discrimination  *85, 88*
    same-sex relationships  *55*
    Desmond Tutu  *91, 136*
disease  *105, 106*
divorce  *74, 75, 76, 77*
Dolly the sheep  *47, 48, 49*
donor insemination (DI)  **33**, *36, 37, 38*, **144**
droughts  *97, 98, 105*
drugs  *62–69*
    Christian attitudes to illegal drugs  *66–67*
    Christian attitudes to legal drugs  *65–66*
    crime and punishment  *133*
    drug-taking in Britain  *64*

    helping drug addicts  *64–65*
    illegal drugs  *64*
    legal drugs  *62–63*
    questions and activities  *67–69*

# E

education  *106*
embryonic research  *34*
emergency aid  *111, 112*
Enniskillen bombing  *119*
ensoulment  **13**, **145**
environment  *96–104*
    Christian attitudes  *100–101*
    environmental problems  *97–98*
    key Christian principles  *96*
    questions and activities  *102–04*
    war and peace  *126*
    what can be done?  *99–100*
equality  *87*
Equality and Human Rights Commission  *84, 86*
Equal Opportunities Commission  *86*
Equal Pay Act (*1970*)  *86*
Eucharist (Holy Communion)  *74*, **76**, **145**
eugenics  *43*
euthanasia  *21–30*
    arguments for and against  *24–25*
    Christian attitudes  *26–27*
    definition  **21**, **145**
    hospice movement  *23–24*
    questions and activities  *27–30*
    sources of morality  *4*
    types  *22–23*
Evans, Rhys  *41, 43*
exam technique  *142–43*
extra-marital sex  **56**, **145**

# F

fair trade  **110**, *111, 112*, **145**
fertility treatment  *32–40*
    arguments for and against  *36*
    Christian attitudes  *36–38*